# Creating a Culture

# Creating a Culture

## THE RESTAURANT MACHINE

• • •

*Nick Vlahos*

ISBN-13: 9781981647408
ISBN-10: 1981647406
Library of Congress Control Number: 2017919214
CreateSpace Independent Publishing Platform
North Charleston, South Carolina

*Unless your organization has a culture of teamwork and respect, where the individuals who show up every day and give their best are valued, your business will slowly fade away.*

# Dedication

● ● ●

*This book would not have been possible without the help of my wife Maria. Her continuous support and encouragement enabled me to pursue my goal of putting my ideas and viewpoints into words.*
*I would also like to dedicate this book to the countless managers out there who, like me, value their employees and strive to see them succeed.*

# The Restaurant Machine

• • •

SUCCESS IN A RESTAURANT IS dependent on many departments working in unison to serve a guest. I view these different departments as gears. These various gears must be properly timed and aligned, to produce optimal output. The desired output for a restaurant machine is to have a great tasting product, timely served by a friendly, knowledgeable staff at a profit. The gears in the restaurant machine are the staff and the departments they maintain. Every gear, every position, in a restaurant is important and will cause the restaurant machine to start failing if not running efficiently. The beauty of a well-oiled restaurant machine is what the guest experiences-- and that is a seamless dining cycle. The finished product. Many guests will never know the complexities of the processes required, to produce their selection. The guest doesn't need to know. All the guest wants is to put their hand on the throttle and have the dining cycle move at their desired pace.

# Table of Contents

The Restaurant Machine · · · · · · · · · · · · · · · · · · · · · · · ix
Preface · · · · · · · · · · · · · · · · · · · · · · · · · · · · · · · · · · xiii

Section I    A Little History of Food-Service Culture · · · · · · · · · · 1
             Why Is Customer Service in Hospitality
             So Important? · · · · · · · · · · · · · · · · · · · · · · · · · 7
             What Is Hospitality? · · · · · · · · · · · · · · · · · · · · · 12
             Who Are You? · · · · · · · · · · · · · · · · · · · · · · · · · 15
             Your Staff Is Your Greatest Asset! · · · · · · · · · · · · · 21
Section II   Boss or Leader? · · · · · · · · · · · · · · · · · · · · · · · 28
             It's All About People Skills · · · · · · · · · · · · · · · · · 28
             You Need a Business Model · · · · · · · · · · · · · · · · · 32
             Optimal Interaction · · · · · · · · · · · · · · · · · · · · · 36
             The Road to Becoming a Leader · · · · · · · · · · · · · · · 46
Section III  It's All About the Team · · · · · · · · · · · · · · · · · · · · 68
             Is Your Work Environment Toxic? · · · · · · · · · · · · · · 74
             The Baby-Blanket Syndrome · · · · · · · · · · · · · · · · 77
             The Farm System · · · · · · · · · · · · · · · · · · · · · · · 79

             About the Author · · · · · · · · · · · · · · · · · · · · · · · 83
             References · · · · · · · · · · · · · · · · · · · · · · · · · · · 85

# Preface

● ● ●

THE ALARM CLOCK BUZZED. I rushed to get dressed to catch up with my father, who was leaving for work. It was 4:30 a.m., and he had to go open the restaurant. There were customers who relied on him for early-morning coffee and breakfast. I was twelve years old, going in to work with my dad during summer vacation. But I knew that if I didn't make it to the car before he pulled away, he wouldn't wait. Well, he did wait on some occasions.

What I remember most of my father at his restaurant was the pleasure he took in providing hospitality. His approach was fundamentally sound: he made every attempt to make sure that guests were happy to come spend their money there, over and over. Thinking back to that diner setting, I see that goodwill exhibited to the guest with a sense of urgency was the ingredient for success. Customer service means willingly going the extra mile for a guest—who will notice this sense of urgency and extra effort. Guests might not tell you, but they will speak of their experience to other people. Good word of mouth will win you more customers. Through my years of working in restaurants and bars, as well as being a customer, I have witnessed an industry which relies on customer service: struggling to satisfy the wants of the guest. In the age of the educated consumer, the restaurant industry must work harder than ever to earn the loyalty of guests. Even more than that, the industry must understand that the guest's expectations are greater than ever before.

Another thing that is greater than ever before is the choice of dining options that the consumer has. Consumers want to feel valued for spending their hard-earned money at any business. They want the entire experience: great food served in a timely manner by an intelligent staff in a welcoming environment. As your customer becomes better and better informed, your business plan must revolve around better training in the art of hospitality as well as product knowledge. Gaining a competitive edge over your competition will boil down to who has better customer service. Who is giving the customer more reasons to come back? The answer is simple: your people. It is the staff. It is the culture!

The way a staff behaves and interacts, amongst itself and its customers, is an important component of the restaurant machine and the focus of "Creating a Culture". Although skills are important, too, they can be taught to individuals who choose to put in the effort to learn. I am referring to something much more valuable than a mere skill set: the business culture and the staff's ability to work as a team. A business's culture is the environment that the staff works within. It cannot be taught in a class. It is not a switch that can be turned on or off. It is something that evolves. It comes down to everyday interactions between management, staff, and guests. These interactions must be genuine and conducted with respect and goodwill.

Do you sense a problem with your business's environment but can't quite put your finger on what it is? Do you sense resistance when you ask for changes to be implemented? Are you having trouble keeping qualified staff members? If you can answer yes to these questions, you probably have a toxic culture. In this book, you will learn not only how to identify the source of the problems but also how rectify them.

At some point in my thirty-five-plus years in this industry, I realized what the true recipe for success for an organization is, and it is not the brick-and-mortar establishment. The first ingredient is the relationship between the management and staff. It is crucial this relationship is positive, with respect being its fundamental base. The next ingredient relies on the first to truly be a great product—just like a great starter dough, like a *biga*, is needed to make a great rustic bread like a ciabatta. This second ingredient is how the business's team interacts with the guest. It must be great customer service delivered with a healthy portion of hospitality.

In this book, I have compiled information that draws from my own success over the years. It is intended to help people in the restaurant business—or any business that relies on building a team. You will learn how to build a team that works within an established culture of teamwork and respect. Owning a diner taught me the business and the importance of customer service in building a loyal guest following. I was also very fortunate to have had some great mentors who taught me how to run a business on a large scale. I see a mentor as someone you work with rather than work for. Most of my knowledge, however, has come from my own observations and, sometimes, even my own mistakes.

To truly excel at customer service, your company's culture and leadership style must be one of humility. I will explain more about this later when we discuss how a manager transitions into a leader. My approach for a successful business focuses on the level of customer service that guests experience. To accomplish that, building a team is the most important objective, as I will later explain, in the restaurant machine.

We can also learn a lot from the history of food service. It's not so much about learning from past mistakes, though we like to think we learn from our own mistakes as well as from those of others. I am referring to not seeing the importance of human interaction between your guests and your team member(s). Everything ultimately comes down to one-on-one interaction; that is the guest's experience. That is the guest's perception. I will briefly reference the history of food service from the street vendors of ancient civilizations to the French Revolution and the present. I believe that customer service will determine the success of a business as we head into tomorrow, as well.

In our digital age, human interaction isn't as prevalent as I remember it growing up. This doesn't mean that you can falter in customer service. It means that for you to differentiate your business from that of your competition, your level of customer service must exceed what your competition is offering.

Managers have the enormous responsibility of assembling and developing a team. They have an even greater responsibility: that of creating a culture, which is a necessary component to a business's success. The way a manager must interact and engage with the staff to succeed is what I call "optimal interaction." Gaining the respect of the team is a prerequisite for a manager to transition into being a leader. I will discuss ways to improve a negative business culture as well as necessary steps in evaluating personnel. I'll discuss something I call the "baby-blanket syndrome," which pertains to employees who work against the establishment of a culture. The "farm system" discussion is about the development and constant rebuilding of a team, which is necessary in such a transitionary business for future growth.

Before we get into the heart of discussion, I want to remind you that this book is about creating the culture that your business needs to truly excel at customer service—not about how to run a business, which is known as operations.

# A Little History of Food-Service Culture

● ● ●

In 2016, the US Bureau of Labor Statistics said that the country had 908,550 food-service supervisors and managers. These managers were responsible for managing just under 12.5 million employees. Get your calculator out for that one. It works out that each manager and supervisor was responsible for about fourteen employees on average. The bureau also predicted that with the continuous growth in population, more people will be going out to eat. That makes perfect sense. It also means that more managers will be needed to manage even more employees so that they can serve even more guests.

In addition, the dual-income household has become more prevalent, according to Howard V. Hayghe, a Bureau of Labor Statistics economist. He traces the changing labor-force characteristics of families since the *Monthly Labor Review* began publication (Hayghe 1990). Half a century ago, most children lived in traditional families, with the husband in the labor force and the wife at home. Over time, this scenario has become the exception rather than the rule. The graph below reflects that this trend continues. In 2016, both husband and wife were employed in 48 percent of married couples. Among such families with children, 61.1 percent had both parents employed (US Department of Labor 2017).

With both parents working, answering the question "What's for dinner?" can be a challenge. There is neither the time nor the inclination for parents to prepare home-cooked meals after a long day at work.

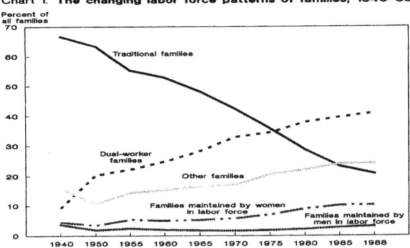

Chart 1. The changing labor force patterns of families, 1940–88

Of course, there are options, with one of them being going out to eat. Eating out, as history has shown us, was at first reserved for travelers. Today it is done out of convenience and as a subtle break from everyday routine. Regardless of if the outing is formal or informal, it still resonates as an event and a treat. Another point for consideration is that eating out occurs in a social setting. More than being interested in just the food, people hope to be entertained while being treated like royalty for the duration of their visit.

However, with the greater frequency of dining out, consumers are becoming more educated about it. They compare and rate you versus your competition. Consumers are smarter, more experienced, and more aware, so they are better able to evaluate you based on criteria such as menu selection and pricing. They are also evaluating you on your ambience and cleanliness. Mostly, though, they evaluate you on your level of service and execution of delivery—and compare it to that of your competition. Just because more people are eating out doesn't mean they will come to you. You must have a system in place that ensures proper and consistent preparation of a product and must also excel at delivering it.

The restaurant and bar business seems a lot easier than what it is. Maybe that's because there are restaurants at every turn. Various concepts are trying to target every niche appetite imaginable. So, who are the people making investments in a start-up restaurant market that has been said to fail in the first year at a 90 percent rate? Well, don't believe this myth. According to a study by H. G. Parsa and his team at Cornell University, the truer failure rate for first-year restaurants was just under 30 percent, though after three years, it's around 60 percent (Parsa 2005).

This study was a snapshot of the Columbus, Ohio, market, but you have probably seen similar numbers in your own neighborhood. A new restaurant opens, and it seems to do well for a while. Then in a year or two, it's closed or under new management. So why do it? Why go into a business where almost two out of three establishments fail within three years? The answer is simple—at least to some. It is one of the greatest businesses to be in if you have a passion for hospitality.

Hospitality is a people business with the goal of making each guest's day a little better. You make money while customers satisfy their basic need for eating and are entertained in a social environment. These businesses also have a relatively low start-up cost compared to other businesses that similarly create an immediate cash flow. It seems simple enough. First you get a business plan together, which, very basically, is a decision on what your target audience is and how you'll tailor your concept to that specific market. Next, menu development and pricing must work with your entire identity while remaining appealing to your target customer. Finally, it is very important to keep the level of motivation running high, because once the design aspect is complete and all the details get hammered out, the real work begins: hiring and training staff.

After the dust settles from the excitement of the initial opening, building business and keeping it is your only lifeline. I remember my father telling me, while I was peeling potatoes at his restaurant when I was twelve, that you had to work very hard to get a customer but must work twice as hard to keep him or her. Customer service, back then, seemed to revolve around pure hustle. Unfortunately, today pure hustle is not enough. This is where most new restauranteurs make their first and most critical mistake—by not properly preparing the staff for execution and delivery of product. They may have good intentions, but they do not have much, if any, experience in how to do this.

You won't get many chances to wow your guests with customer service, so a great team needs to be in place from the get-go. An easy way to explain this is with a basic math principle: the zero-product property. But first, let me repeat that this book intends to show the importance of a staff that cares and constantly tries to provide great product and customer service. This is the culture—and it is the key to building business and keeping it! Guests need to feel appreciated, and they must see the value in what they are spending.

The zero-product property is that anything multiplied by zero is zero. We all learned this in math class at an early age. Let's say that service at your establishment is mediocre. Yet you serve your menu with fancy forks and those trendy plates under expensive lighting. But if you multiply those with mediocre customer service, the result is zero! Without good customer service, your result will always be zero, and you will not be able to build business. The effect may not show up right away, depending on how bad the service actually is. In the restaurant industry, we call this the "honeymoon period"—when a concept first opens and gets to spread its wings and fly, or it crashes and burns. Customers want to see and experience new concepts, so this is your chance to make the best first impression possible! They will give you a try. Are you prepared to rock this first-time customer to get him or her to come back? Have you given him or her a reason to come back?

*Creating a Culture* will explain how to avoid the zero-product-multiplication scenario for service businesses. Not only does the culture of your establishment determine whether you avoid the zero-product property, but also, if you provide exceptional customer service, your positive results will be magnified.

In my experience, the growth and longevity of a restaurant depends on three general properties. I refer to them as "the restaurant machine." First, you satisfy guests by providing what they desire. Second, you satisfy owners or investors by running an efficient and profitable operation. Third and most important, you do everything within a positive team environment. This is by far the most important cog in the restaurant machine. Restaurants are first and foremost customer-service-based businesses. Dealing with the public requires many skills, a certain level of professionalism, and hospitality from the team providing the service. This is what continues to bring customers back again and again.

*Creating a Culture* digs deep on how to change an existing culture and also how to instill a culture in a start-up. Change always happens from the top: management. This is another key to success. I will discuss a managers' development from recruitment through various challenges they will face. I focus on the importance of building a team—a melting pot of personalities and employees from various backgrounds. It is most important to have leadership that binds the team to work as one family as it provides a great product with great service.

Many restaurant managers have a strong knowledge of restaurant operations and know the details of their unit. There are many different management styles; all can be very effective based on the needs of a specific concept in a specific market. Your team needs to understand that the true basis of great customer service is a sincere interest in helping the guest by sweating the small details.

Let's compare a few concepts. A bustling diner in the inner city builds its reputation and success on pure hustle and good food. If its customer has only an hour to travel there, order, eat, pay, and return to work, there is no room for error. The diner satisfies the customer's basic need to eat, but it does so in a fulfilling way. If this is a frequent customer, there might be small talk or light conversation with the staff or other patrons, and he or she will leave happy and satisfied.

Now let's take a concept like finer dining, where customers are looking for more than just satisfying their desire to eat. They are also satisfying their desire to be entertained and served. They are looking for pampering. The hustle of the diner we just discussed has no place in this concept. This concept demands a form of customer service that caters to a more elegant, unrushed experience. Entertaining a guest does not necessarily mean having music, dancing, or sporting events on TV. It could just mean amazing food and drink selections served in that cozy booth in a dimly-lit room—a romantic experience. Regardless of the reasons that people go out to eat, guests expect a stress-free experience to satisfy their desire to eat and be served.

Managers are trained to follow the system set in place at their units. In my experience owning and managing at a variety of restaurants, I've generally seen no system in place to aid in leading the staff. Unfortunately, there are also few leaders in the field who can develop other managers. In lieu of true leadership, the managers are taught how to *drive* the staff. We all learn from someone; hopefully the manager's mentor instilled in him or her the importance of the staff and why they should be valued.

Your employees are your biggest assets. They are on the front line, interacting with the customers. You will see the difference between inspiring your staff members and driving them. An inspired team will want to do the best job and understand that it is an integral part of the business. The key word here is "want." The way to get employees to *want* to do something means leading your team—not driving it. I mentioned that *Creating a Culture* will discuss the qualities that a manager needs to transition into being a leader. "Leader" is not a title you give yourself. It is a title that your team gives you.

I'll also go into the importance of having a management team in place whose members complement each other. I'll address the many staffing challenges that managers face, from hiring and promoting to developing and identifying personality types. Managers must be able to deal with a melting pot of egos daily. Unfortunately, at times, managers have to deal with long-standing employees who are reluctant to change (the baby-blanket syndrome). Then there is optimal interaction—the way you talk and interact with your staff for best results. I've observed many management styles through the years and bring you the best and most effective techniques that I have found to transform a restaurant from a losing business to a growing and thriving one.

## WHY IS CUSTOMER SERVICE IN HOSPITALITY SO IMPORTANT?

Customer service—the interaction between customer and staff member— is key in any hospitality business. Food service is a type of complex retail operation. Unlike some retail businesses, where you can just turn on the lights and you're ready for the first customer, restaurants are a little more involved. Staff members show up and ready their stations; the front-of-the-house staff starts detailing the sales floor. Everything the guest sees and touches must be clean and organized. The restaurant retail concept relies heavily on providing a great experience, and that starts with first impressions.

I see the front of the house as the sales floor, and the back of the house, the kitchen, as the restaurant's production department. The responsibility of the chef is enormous. Let's face it—if the quality of the food is poor, it really won't matter what kind of service is provided; the customer will not return! The capable person running the kitchen must be recognized as a necessary leadership cog in the restaurant machine. There must be a cohesiveness between the front of the house and the back of the house. The only way to perfect the customer-service experience is through a team effort between the sales team and the production team. If those areas are strained and not running in unison, it will create a tension in the environment. Any stressors in your business's operations will eventually be felt by your customer.

To better appreciate the importance of customer service, and where it is heading, is to take a look at food service history. As ancient civilizations grew, so did the demand for food to feed the masses. In China,

Mesopotamia, Greece, and Rome, the demand for prepared foods also grew. Greece had marketplaces where vendors could sell their goods, including imported things brought from abroad. Buyers no longer had to depend on sustaining themselves only from their own farms or even nearby farmlands. They could buy ingredients grown by others or even prepared and ready to eat—bread, for example.

Not all people, such as laborers and traveling traders, had the resources to prepare their own food. Taverns and street vendors were very popular. A tavern usually had a large, common table for people to sit at, but there was no menu selection. People ate what the tavern keeper prepared. Of course, it was likely that the better bowl of soup in town made for a busier establishment. Strangers came together in a social environment to enjoy a meal, but more than that, there was conversation and laughter. There was human interaction, and it was entertaining.

Here we see the concept of customer service in its infancy—fulfilling the basic need to eat and drink while someone is served and entertained. Now there's a concept! The working class would patronize these taverns, while the wealthy took a different road. They would have their own personal cooks to prepare daily meals and a staff to serve them. The wealthy would host dinner events, inviting their guests to these private social gatherings to eat and be served.

The modern restaurant originated in eighteenth-century France, right after the French Revolution. According to Lynne Olver, "It relaxed the legal rights of guilds that (since the Middle Ages) were licensed by the king to control specific foods (e.g., the Patissiers, Rotisseurs, Charcutiers) and created a hungry, middle-class customer base who relished the ideals of egalitarianism (as in, anyone who could pay the price could get the same meal). Entrepreneurial French chefs were quick to capitalize on this market. Menus, offering dishes individually portioned, priced and prepared to order, were introduced to the public for the first time" (Olver 2000).

Food service underwent a revolution of its own with the rise of the restaurant concept. It was new to be served at a private table after ordering from a menu that offered a choice of selections. This was the time when the bourgeois, or middle class, blossomed. Eating began taking on social significance, like an art. Early gastronomic writings exhibited a great appreciation for the finer things in life, like eating well. People who could afford to eat this way relished the opportunity to display their wealth and style in an effort to climb the social ladder.

Eating is such an integral part of our daily lives. Food does so much more than provide basic sustenance. It literally defines us and our cultures. Eating is even a social event at home, like having dinner with your family and staying abreast of events in each other's lives.

Eating brings us a sense of satisfaction and relaxation, but it has even had religious significance as well. Here is a personal example. I grew up in a traditional Greek household. During Easter, the most sacred Greek Orthodox holiday, certain traditions governed which foods we were allowed to eat and when. During Lent, we observed periods of fasting where a vegan diet was observed. Easter Sunday celebrates the end of fasting, and a large feast is prepared.

Fasting and feasting seem to go hand in hand—not just in Greek culture. Most cultures associate food with religion and social significance. During the month of Ramadan, Muslims fast during daylight hours and eat only before dawn or after sunset. These traditions are passed down from generation to generation as a reminder of the culture from their motherland. The Jewish culture observes kosher rules that outline which foods can be eaten as well as how they are to be prepared and by whom. Many followers of Hinduism and Buddhism follow a strict credo of nonviolence toward other living creatures and therefore eat a vegetarian diet.

Restaurants must provide a welcoming and hospitable environment to try to make their customers feel at home. A make-yourself-at-home mentality combined with the hospitality of your staff will have your customer feeling like family.

What does it take to make customers feel at home? When you invite guests to your own home, you treat them like family with warmth and friendliness. It's the same with your customers. They are invited too—you're open for business. When they feel comfortable, they can become frequent diners. If they don't, you'll never see them again. In early restaurants like taverns, there was little need for customer service; there was just a need to feed. With increased competition, customer service arose as a by-product that could differentiate one business from another.

Once the modern concept of a sit-down restaurant arose, suddenly there was a need to have people in place to serve a customer his or her selected menu item. The public, of course, recognized that the level of service received varied from restaurant to restaurant. It's only logical that people would patronize establishments that made them feel valued and at home.

It sounds very simple, this restaurant business. Customers ordering menu items and having them delivered to their tables is nothing revolutionary. It's been happening since the French Revolution. But, in my opinion, customer service—customer engagement—has become paramount for success.

Ray Kroc changed things in the restaurant business —not as much by what McDonald's sold but rather by how the business was executed. The beauty was not the burger wrapped in wax paper or the fries. It was in the vision of franchising. With franchising came another challenge, and that was product consistency. Ray Kroc wanted to have a cookie cutter system in place that would produce identical products at every location. The way he accomplished that was to persuade investors to buy into his vision of franchising through ownership.

It is difficult to think of a product that revolutionized the restaurant world. At the St. Louis World's Fair in the early 1900s, French's introduced yellow mustard and served on a hot dog for the first time (French's 2014). But we'd hardly call it revolutionary. According to Wikipedia,

Archeological excavations in the Indus Valley (Indian Subcontinent) have revealed that mustard was cultivated there. That civilization existed until about 1800 BC. The Romans experimented with the preparation of mustard as a condiment. They mixed unfermented grape juice (the must) with ground mustard seeds (called sinapis) to make "burning must," *mustum ardens*—hence "must ard."

The hot dog is just a sausage served in a vessel of bread. How long have sausages been around? Hot dog historian Bruce Kraig says, "The Germans always ate the dachshund sausages with bread. Since the sausage culture is German, it is likely that Germans introduced the practice of eating the dachshund sausages, which we today know as the hot dog, nestled in a bun" (Kraig 2016), but no one is certain. In any case, it could have been so that people could eat sausages without burning themselves.

It is near impossible to trace back to who was the first to discover a food item. Archeologists are still debating when cooking food originated. Regardless, knowing when cooking first occurred isn't as important as knowing how it has evolved. It hasn't fundamentally changed all that much—raw product is cooked through. But now we also have "secret recipes" with particular combinations of ingredients, spices and procedures.

There's a lot of copying in the restaurant business, but that's OK. You don't have to reinvent the wheel. All you need to do is take someone else's business model and replicate it. You can make subtle changes if you like. The beauty of the restaurant business is that success does not hinge on creating a cutting-edge product. It does hinge, however, on the execution, preparation, and delivery of that product. The customer will patronize the establishment that excels at execution. Businesses that are unable to execute will eventually get weeded out in a competitive market. In a customer-service-oriented business, value is created in the mind of the consumer by the level of hospitality displayed by your staff—as well as your prices.

# What Is Hospitality?

According to Wikipedia, "Hospitality refers to the relationship between a guest and a host, wherein the host receives the guest with goodwill, including the reception and entertainment of guests, visitors and strangers." What is goodwill? The *Merriam-Webster Dictionary* says that it "is a kind, helpful, or friendly feeling or attitude." How does this pertain to the food-service industry?

You give an enormous responsibility to your front-of-the-house staff to interact with customers and sell your prepared product to them. While your staff members interact with guests, you expect them to have a friendly and kind attitude. Your ultimate success hinges on every employee's ability to do this, day in and day out, with every guest. That, in a nutshell, is why you need to create a culture.

There is no cookie-cutter method to teach hospitality because every team member is unique and has his or her own personality. For a customer to feel hospitality, the server must also have a sincere approach. A smile cannot be faked. Customers can sense insincerity. This must be communicated to the staff, because its members must understand that they are in the hospitality business.

In the restaurant world, there usually is a meeting with the staff before the scheduled shift starts. It is called a pre-shift or roundup. This is a sales meeting, of a sort, consisting of reviewing need-to-know information. One error that managers commonly make is not having this meeting in the kitchen. Your culture must be that of a team—so include the back of the house! During a pre-shift meeting, ask your staff to explain hospitality. You will get a mix of responses. It is difficult to explain, because it is subject to interpretation. There is one thing that your staff members will all agree on: when they receive it, they feel it. And feeling something is real.

How the product you sell is served to the customer determines the level of hospitality the guest perceives. The staff must understand that the goal of the business is to try to make sure every guest feels hospitality. The importance of guest perception cannot be stressed enough.

Your staff members must understand that the way they interact with guests determines whether the guests will be comfortable or standoffish. This is where things get challenging, because you need to maintain an environment where your employees strive to give great customer service. Your restaurant environment combined with the goodwill of your staff is your culture.

So, how do you establish a culture? Restaurants usually have employee handbooks with a code of ethics. They emphasize expected behaviors and areas of responsibility. Handbooks may help managers govern staff, but the problem with guidelines is that they try to explain which behaviors are acceptable and which are not. This allows room for interpretation and gray areas, because you can't predict every possible scenario. Acts of aggression and harassment are obvious and easy to identify. If proper behavior is not followed, certain disciplinary actions, including termination, can follow. How about just performing at a mediocre, lazy level? This interpretation is subjective. Interpretation by a manager who is self-centered and disrespectful of others will be biased. Staff members who behave against the guidelines, or in the gray area, work against a positive environment.

You may have a mission statement at your restaurant; mission statements often tell a little story—who you are, what you do, why you do it, and how it should be done. Your business is a food-service operation that sells a product for a profit through great service, but it is the "how" that can be vague. What does "offering great service" mean? How do you measure that? Does everyone on your staff even know what selling great service through hospitality is all about? This is a subjective topic. Everyone has a different interpretation of what bad, good, and great service are. Does the staff know that service is an intangible product that it should be selling? Customers are consciously and subconsciously comparing you to your competition.

Another vague concept is "treating each other with respect"—a phrase often nestled somewhere in a code of ethics. Obviously, blatant acts of aggression are violations. How about helping teammates when they are overwhelmed? Do your teammates want to help each other to succeed and aid in each other's development? The willingness of your staff members to help each other to be successful is a benchmark of respect. Without team members that respect each other and work together in conjunction with good food and great service, your business will never exceed customer expectations. Exceeding customer expectations requires a team effort and must be the focal point of every mission statement within the hospitality industry. It cannot be achieved without a positive culture of respect and teamwork in place at your establishment.

My definition of culture is quite basic—like something out of an elementary-school social-studies class: the culture is the way your team behaves according to the way they were taught. I want to add that culture is also the way your staff behaves when no one is watching. I am not referring to being taught something like a procedure—such as how to work the point-of-sale system. I am referring to behavior within the interaction among staff members—in other words, proper workplace etiquette: things like watching one's tone when speaking to others, cordiality, and respect. Those traits are more easily taught if the trainee is put in a positive environment from the get-go. The trainee will think that this is the way things are at your place of business.

Your team learns how to act through interaction with management. Culture is the environment created by people interacting and working together. The culture, or behavior, that your employees learn is from the existing environment, which could have a negative or positive atmosphere. Establishing a positive culture, with good people working together well, is important in any business. In the hospitality industry, it is crucial. Your staff's behavior will have a direct impact on the guest experience. How does your staff behave when no one is watching or listening? How does it behave on those busy days when everyone's stress levels are running high?

Everyone's top priority at your place of business should be to build business. The food-service industry is extremely competitive, and to survive in it, you must have a good reputation and a loyal following. The good-reputation part sounds easy from the outside looking in. Those on the inside see the formula for success as good food with great service, every day, to every guest. Every day, to every guest? That sounds impossible, especially since you are relying on the many different personalities of people to accomplish this. This is where your established culture comes into play. This is why you are looking for the right team chemistry—a team that naturally has goodwill. It must have a positive and energetic attitude. This starts with recruitment and development of all the staff, starting with the management. Management establishes the culture that creates a good reputation. Without a positive culture, you run the risk of chasing away customers and great employees.

Customers have more restaurant choices today than ever before. It seems that everywhere you turn, a new restaurant concept is opening. Some spend exorbitant amounts on technology and decor. But I have noticed that as technology grows, customer service shrinks. In some concepts, people are not needed to take orders—the customer can order from the table on a tablet device and have the food delivered. These customers don't want a salesperson; they just want a delivery person. You can even pay electronically at the table. Where is the human element of interaction heading? If people want to eat cafeteria-style, they can go find a buffet where they have limited interaction with the server getting their drinks.

## WHO ARE YOU?

Customer service was the focus of the mom-and-pop stores of yesterday. That was when hard work, good food, and good service were the ingredients for success. So, how does a restaurant gain the competitive edge to differentiate itself from the competition? Before you answer that, think about this: Who are you, and whom are you looking to attract as a customer?

What is your identity? This question confuses many restauranteurs because many times they try to cater to all appetites. This approach has its drawbacks. As a consumer, I wouldn't want to see someone eating a hot dog where I just ordered a fifty-dollar steak. That would be confusing because your identity is simply your customers' expectations when they choose to dine with you. This is important for restaurant owners to understand because an identity must be established. It is not enough to say that your concept is a deli, diner or full service. It is equally important for your customer to know where your concept lies on, what I refer to as, the luxury scale. The luxury scale is directly related to guest perception. This perception is based on the quality of food, the level of service and the cost for that experience. Your guest will have certain expectations, based on where you claim to be on this scale. When that guest walks through your door, they will notice the atmosphere and the friendliness of the staff. From that point forward it's all about menu selections and the quality of those items, to the staff and the level of service they provide. When you're creating your identity, guest expectations are extremely important to know before selecting your staff. The higher you would like to see your business on the luxury scale, the more disciplined and refined the culture must be. If a business wants to market itself as "fine dining," the guest experience must be near flawless every time. To accomplish that, it takes a level of experience and passion that is more than mere order taking and delivery.

Here is a simple example of how the luxury scale is relevant in the food-service industry. Chicken Caesar salad is a simple-enough dish that can be found at any dining level. Let's start with the lower-priced end of the scale. You walk into a diner to grab a quick bite. You may or may not get greeted by a host. More than likely, you will seat yourself unless you are directed to a table by a passing server. When your server arrives at your booth, you may or may not exchange pleasantries with him or her, and the dining process begins. The food and beverage order is taken immediately: an iced tea and Chicken Caesar salad.

In about a minute, your beverage is delivered. Your salad will probably consist of a sliced, grilled chicken breast over a bed of romaine lettuce tossed in a Caesar dressing that more than likely came out of a gallon jug. It would then be garnished with some croutons and parmesan cheese. The room is probably well lit with windows and lighting. The background sound is muffled conversation, because the tables are close together. Other noise includes dishes clanking when they're bussed and maybe conversations or order calling between servers and cooks.

My father's first restaurant, a little diner in the city, was like that. The servers would call their orders in to the kitchen; there weren't even tickets. Controlling the chaos was the key to success. The only way to learn how to control the chaos is to experience it. The typical diner's environment is quick paced. On the table, you find your silverware, probably rolled in a paper napkin, possibly set on a placemat printed with advertisements. You'll also find ketchup and mustard there, maybe in some sort of caddy with salt and pepper shakers and sugar packets.

What menu expectations do guests have when they see ketchup and mustard bottles on the table? I would think of hamburgers and french fries. How about the servers? What are your expectations of their knowledge level? You expect them to have basic knowledge of the menu, as far as what the ingredients are and how things are served. You would expect them to know the daily soups and specials as well. Your overall expectations of the meal and service are satisfied if the chicken breast is grilled correctly and sits atop a bed of crisp, fresh romaine lettuce with a decent dressing and croutons that aren't stale. The service needs to be quick and efficient, with a nice, smiling server.

These features would put the perceived value in line with the cost of the Chicken Caesar salad. Remember, as a restaurant owner in a competitive market, you always need to be aware of what your competition is doing as far as pricing and service. Your guests sure are.

Heading to the other end of the scale, what are your expectations for that same Chicken Caesar salad at an upscale, fine-dining restaurant? The luxury customer desires a level of pampering when it comes to service and attentiveness. It starts right when you walk in the front door and are immediately greeted by a host or maybe even a maître d'. These people are very professional and polished as they escort you to your table. The pace is unrushed. The server approaches to greet and introduce her or himself. This is where just service with a smile is not enough. Guests at a finer-dining restaurant seek a more memorable experience.

In the pursuit of exceeding guests' expectations, avoid branding your business at the higher end of the luxury scale if your product or service is mediocre. The finer-dining server is very knowledgeable on menu selections, including ingredients and preparation. He or she may be a veteran of the industry. Next, there might be a wine sommelier stopping by your table if there is an interest in the wine list, along with any wines featured for the evening. The sommelier can also answer any questions regarding pairing. The server delivers the beverages in an efficient yet unobtrusive manner—polished. He or she goes over the evening's features in detail and follows the steps of service, which are used to guide the guest through the suggested dining flow to optimize guest experience.

We will take the Chicken Caesar salad as in our previous scenario. Now the guest's expectations are far greater for this salad. The chicken breast should be of top quality, from a free-range chicken fed an organic, non-GMO diet. The romaine lettuce most likely be both organically grown and locally sourced, fresh and crisp. The dressing, which is the most important part, along with the croutons, should be made from scratch. Ideally the dressing and salad should be made and assembled tableside by the pantry chef. The salad will be topped with the highest-grade Parmesan cheese, freshly shaved. Knowledgeable customers normally seek out such products at top restaurants. Customer perception is key, especially when it comes to fine dining. It's all about the presentation, because we eat with our eyes before the food ever touches our mouths.

The environment has ambient lighting, with the background sound consisting of a piano player or soft house music. The mood is relaxing and unrushed. Tables are spacious and dressed with linen, and they may have candles or other intimate lighting. They are very uncluttered. Other menu selections also include high-quality ingredients.

The Chicken Caesar salad ordered at the fine-dining restaurant can fetch three or four times the price of the casual diner's version. The difference of perceived value involves the entire experience. From the warm welcome at the host area upon arrival to the special attention of the server, the guest feels valued. The sommelier suggesting wine pairings in addition to the pantry chef preparing salad tableside definitely creates value as well as entertainment. With this whole package of experiences, the guest justifies the premium paid to the fine-dining restaurant.

The diner and the fine-dining establishment are on opposite ends of the luxury scale. Many concepts fall in between—like pub style, various bistro levels, and upscale casual. Each one of these concepts is trying to attract or select a particular customer, using pricing as an invisible stanchion. As I've shown, it's very important not only to know your identity but also to know where you want to stand on this scale. For this, you must know who your competition is. The best way to know the competition is to shop it. Remember the importance of customer perception. Your customers eat at your competition, so you must be better than your competition!

From the inns, taverns, and street vendors of the ancient cities to the time of the French Revolution, when restaurants as we know them today were born, customer service has undergone an evolution. And so have the customers. Today's customers are knowledgeable and very interested in finding restaurants that can satisfy their desires and provide memorable experiences. They can find mediocrity anywhere. They expect to be pampered, and if you fail to meet that expectation, you'll lose them to your competition. No business can weather that. If the historical trend continues, customer service will only become more important. The hospitality business cannot skimp on customer service. Your staff is whom your guests engage with, so your staff culture must be great.

It is almost pointless to debate whose food is better when you get to the level of high-end dining featuring the top culinary artists. There, all the food is spectacular. I want to take this to the other end of the spectrum and point out, however, that no restaurant can sell a "bad" anything and have any chance of keeping its doors open. Your customer will visit you once, maybe twice, before dropping you. You always want to be one of your customer's top two choices. Customers are very fickle, and with so many options available, it takes only one bad experience for them to remove you from their go-to list. The goal is to make sure that the guest has a relaxing and pleasurable experience, not a stressful one.

In the restaurant business, competition has narrowed the food-vendor playing field as well. In various regions, there are only a few companies left who supply restaurants. Similar concepts are typically supplied with the same product sold under different labels and packaging, maybe the same product with slight variations. Remember that restaurant concepts copy each other. For example, it's the toppings and bread they're served on that make each burger unique. The reality is, the burger patties are probably all the same, just out of differently labeled boxes, unless they are serving prime meat like *wagyu* or *Piedmontese*.

Similar concepts and identities mimic each other because they are all trying to attract the same customer. Unless you are located in a bustling tourist area, you are relying on the patronage of your local suburbia. You are relying on repeat business from your base customer for survival, and that is what your competitor is also striving for. Competition is a beautiful thing for the consumer. Similar concepts offer incentives for a customer's patronage, like discounts and coupons. For the consumer, who is going out to eat somewhere anyway, why not patronize a restaurant that is giving an incentive? Who doesn't want to save money? And consumers are educating themselves by experiencing what the different restaurants offer. They can then compare you to your competition. This is a contest that you must win. The situation also creates customers that have become conscious of what they want to pay. They expect an upscale dining experience for moderate pricing and will actively seek out establishments that provide it with incentives.

## YOUR STAFF IS YOUR GREATEST ASSET!

Building business is your lifeline to survival. However, we won't discuss profitability in depth because that is the goal of owners and managers. The customer doesn't care how much profit the owners or shareholders make, and it has little to do with establishing a culture. Unfortunately, in the restaurant industry, there is no foolproof formula for success. Building business should lead to increasing sales, which should equate to greater profitability, but the reality is that great food and great service might still not be enough to ensure it. Costs are a contributing factor, including product and labor costs. Controlling the costs of your products goes hand in hand with portioning and rotating which limits waste; control these controllables.

To build business, creating a loyal customer base is the key. Many times over the years, I have observed restaurants putting their effort into seeking new business. That's great as long as your fundamentals are already solid—that is, being great at the basics of execution and delivery of product. What you do not want to do is fumble when it is busy. You cannot invite new guests—or existing ones—into your business and not execute. You will give your first-time guests a terrible first impression, and you also risk stressing out your occasional guests, which could send them to your competition.

If you want to increase your business, focus on the guests who are already patronizing your establishment, and do not disappoint them. Your staff recognizes the occasional and frequent diners. Get to know their names. Treat them like family and offer hospitality. For the most part, people favor a select few restaurants. They have their favorite neighborhood restaurant where they are loyal customers, the place close to home where they take their families. They might run into neighbors and friends there. And they choose these establishments based on their perceived value and comfort. Perception is everything. Your menu fare's cost must be in line with your guest's perceived value, as I previously mentioned when I discussed the luxury scale. There is also a level of comfort and familiarity that is critically needed if you want to create a loyal guest.

It is important that the staff identify these occasional but regular diners. Staff members are the ones who interact with guests and ensure that their experiences are favorable. The culture of your establishment and the way your staff interacts with guests has more to do with creating guest loyalty and retention than your menu does. Sure, you must have menu items that will satisfy guests' taste buds. Each guest, for example, is likely to have a short list of places to get breakfast, dinner and drinks, and for special occasions. You need to make sure that you are at the top of your guests' lists so that they come to you habitually and become regulars. You want to be their first choice because you make them feel at home and valued.

Success, for most restaurants, relies on creating repeat customers or regular diners. Take your own personal experiences and choices. Think about the reasons that you select one restaurant over another. For example, you probably would like your breakfast restaurant to be close to home. But there might be a half-dozen restaurants within a fifteen-minute drive from your residence. Why did you pick your go-to spot? Convenience? But you won't patronize the closest establishment if it has problems with food or service. How many bad experiences does a customer endure before she or he blacklists a restaurant and passes it on the way to the competition?

When customers leave your business, they should feel some level of satisfaction. Well, you hope it is satisfaction. Bad experiences are subjective. There are customers who might not return if the room is too dark or too loud. This goes back to your identity and the type of customer you are trying to attract. For example, a sports bar probably has TVs on the walls and serves pub-style food. The environment is usually loud, with noise from both people and audio. A customer's complaint of a bad experience due to the noise level would be unfortunate, but that's what a sports bar is. A customer complaint like this is aimed at the restaurant's identity. Unless patrons at a table are yelling obscene language or acting belligerent, this is its desired atmosphere.

Here's an example that goes to the heart of a restaurant's culture and a reason that many establishments fail. Let's say you were dining out with some friends and placed your orders with the server. Everything was fine up until then; the server seemed a little rushed. The restaurant was kind of busy but not packed. The server delivered your drinks, and your table was content. You conversed for a while and then realized that your order was taking too long. Your drinks were running dry, and you hadn't seen the server for a while. *That's OK*, you thought. *The place is a little busy, so orders will take a little longer.* What a mediocre word "OK" is to describe an experience!

Then the food came. Great. Then you quickly realized that your order was incorrect. You ordered your steak medium rare, but you cut into it and saw no pink. It might have been cooked correctly at medium rare, but as it sat under a heat lamp, it progressed to well done. After the rest of your party had been eating for five minutes, the server made an appearance to check on everyone. That's an awfully long time sitting idle—you almost forgot who your server was, because you only saw him or her twice. You told your server the problem with your food, and you watched them roll their eyes, annoyed. The server grabbed your plate, and you heard him or her enter the kitchen, screaming at the cooks that they screwed up the order.

The server eventually came back to the table to tell you that they were cooking another one—with no apology, no concern on their part. You looked around, and the rest of your party was more than halfway done eating. The stress made the whole table feel uncomfortable. Ah, here came your plate. You cut into it, and it was rare. They rushed it, and now it was undercooked. Now you were angry and annoyed, and you told your server that you wanted to see the manager.

After a few minutes, the manager approached with a demeanor that gave the impression that you just interrupted whatever they were doing. You explained the problem, knowing the manager had already been briefed. The manager asked if you would like the steak thrown back on the grill, and you said no as you looked around the table at your companions, who were finishing their meals. The manager said that they would take it off the bill as he or she grabbed your plate and walked away. Could it get any more impersonal than that? So uncaring, so lacking in positive culture.

Is this how your employees behave when no one is watching? Where is the goodwill? This interaction between staff and guest is the most important component of hospitality. So now this table pays and leaves. A problem occurred, but the management failed to make any attempt that the patrons could see to correct the mishap. Sure, you can say that the server also failed; however, the manager has the authority to fix matters. The table that just walked out of the restaurant didn't feel valued. Someone from the table probably felt insulted—and definitely embarrassed, if that person was the one who recommended that restaurant. The anger harbored by the guest has created an enemy of the restaurant. The guests at that table will tell everyone what a horrible place that restaurant is. This is not good for building a positive reputation or a loyal customer.

This is a scenario all businesses want to avoid. Any aspect of the dining experience that's perceived as negative will hinder future loyalty. This might even include a middle-of-the-road experience—that perception of "OK." This is where service is only one step above that of a talking vending machine and the food is mediocre at best. Value is a perceived feeling that your guests experience as they pay their tab. You can't have your guests leave your place of business with anything but a good experience.

That is not the way to get repeat customers. Those regular customers are the ones that pull you through on the slower days of the week.

Your energy must be focused on developing your staff in the art of hospitality through service. The first step in developing your staff is to set an example. Always know that your competition is ready and waiting to capture the guests that you lose when you can't satisfy their wants and needs.

It takes time to change a business's culture. It is not as simple as flicking a switch. But here is what is that simple: identifying and acknowledging that your business has a cultural problem. Where do you start to fix a negative or toxic culture?

I remember talking with the owner of a business I managed about how to approach problems with good time management. Every day he would sit at his desk and go through voice messages first, writing down that day's tasks and prioritizing them by urgency. Then he addressed those "first and immediately," as he put it. First and immediately. This struck a chord with me, not only regarding managing time but managing everything.

His daily, disciplined approach reminded me of the "filling a bucket with rocks" metaphor, which you may know. This example of life balance begins with an empty bucket on a table that signifies what we need to get done in a day. Next to the bucket are three piles—one of rocks, one of pebbles, and one of sand—representing the various challenges and responsibilities we encounter daily. The challenge is to fit them all into the bucket. The larger rocks represent the most important or urgent matters. The pebbles represent less urgent ones, and the sand represents trivial matters. The solution to the problem is to fill the bucket with the larger stones first, then add the smaller pebbles, and finally add sand. They will not all fit otherwise.

The bucket-with-rocks example applies to tackling the cultural problem at your business too. Take the bucket that is your culture and identify the biggest obstacles to change—the big rocks. A negative environment at your place of business is fueled by negative employees. The first step is to identify the influencers on your staff; they are the ones who dominate their social surroundings by being loud and intimidating. Such a person is typically a manager or veteran decision-maker. Influencers like these may have created the negative culture, or they allow the current one to continue.

If you are serious about changing the work environment, you must be prepared to shake things up a bit. You cannot have a positive culture with mean and bitter people working in it, so the influencers must be your first shake-up. You expect them to adjust their attitude and adhere to changes, or they'll have to go. Unfortunately, some people are unable to change, leaving you only one option.

In attacking the cultural problem at your business, you start with the rocks. The rocks in a restaurant are the managers or decision-makers in charge. Your management team must be the catalyst for change. Without a solid management team in your bucket—the rocks—you will never be able to get to fitting the pebbles in—the staff.

To succeed, your restaurant machine must be well oiled. You must have a positive environment that, first and most important, is based on respect and teamwork. It should be an environment of individuals that are cordial with one another and want to ensure success for each teammate. The next area of importance is staff development. To establish a positive culture, your team must have the chemistry to willingly work together. You need an environment where the staff displays goodwill through teamwork and has the attitude that no fellow team member will fail. They must behave that way when no one is watching. Better development and training of the staff is the recipe for any business's success. What it means for the staff to be better is that its members can control their areas of responsibility better. Good execution becomes easier, and even when the place is busy, there are no problems and no staff member is overwhelmed. That is my description of a well-oiled restaurant machine.

Of course, to accomplish this, you must retain your staff. You must have a positive culture of teamwork and respect at your business to keep good employees.

# Boss or Leader?

● ● ●

FOR A MANAGER IN ANY industry, walking a mile in your employee's shoes is the only way to understand what his or her position truly entails. You also understand the big picture of the restaurant machine better and appreciate the importance of every single employee's responsibility—every cog. Take your dishwasher, for example. Try serving food when there are no clean dishes, glasses, or silverware. It is very important to have that cog of the restaurant machine engaged and running efficiently. The dishwasher might seem like an insignificant cog in the machine, but the machine will lock up and freeze if that cog is not working properly.

## IT'S ALL ABOUT PEOPLE SKILLS

A restaurant manager's greatest asset is the ability to deal with a diverse group of people—a degree in psychology might make more sense for someone in that position. The melting pot of egos that must be managed on a team is extensive. Even dealing with the public takes a lot of social skills—like patience, listening, and not jumping to conclusions when dealing with an upset customer. You must know when to adopt the "customer is always right" mentality. Whether you can see an irritated guest's point or not, something happened that caused the irritation. This is when your best people skills must come into play. It's about listening, which is more than just hearing. It is understanding what the real problem is. What is your customer really trying to say?

*The most important single ingredient in the formula of
success is the knack of getting along with people.*

THEODORE ROOSEVELT

People skills are what separate the good managers from the mediocre, and you want the good ones when trying to instill and build a positive culture. Over the years, you have probably noticed people who just have a natural ability to speak and are better able to deal with people in general. Even more important than how you speak with the public is how you interact with them. You shouldn't be in the service industry if you cannot be sincere in your demeanor. Most guests are bright enough to tell the difference between people who are being fake, rather than sincere when they handle issues and complaints.

People skills improve with more exposure. If you are in in the hospitality business, you must deal with people; you will not be successful or have longevity unless you continuously hone your skills in interfacing with the public. The reality is that some people you will encounter are just not nice. But for the most part, it isn't personal—that's just who they are. Hopefully the manager knows how to respond in these situations, because being rude and disrespectful to someone who's not nice won't build your business or set a good example for other employees. If the manager doesn't care or be respectful, why should the employees?

Following par lists or doing inventory and scheduling can be taught to just about anyone, but a manager must be great at understanding and dealing with personalities. The way issues get resolved ultimately rests with management. The problem with that is, the issues are not always apparent. This is where the knowledge, training, and awareness of your manager comes into play—the manager's business sense and savvy. It's unfortunate that not many managers have a true understanding of the restaurant business. Sure, all managers think they know the business; they are very good at running around, putting out little fires—a problem here, a problem there. This is just putting Band-Aids on small problems, like an incorrect order at table, and using duct tape to hold things together, like employee drama. Managers can never lead if they are constantly reacting to those situations.

Great management is underrated. It seems like such a simple job that anyone can do it. How hard can running a shift be? The business model is very simple to explain. You need a manager present on the floor in the event managerial functions are needed at the computer. A manager might see that help is needed somewhere and jump in and lend a hand. It might be at the expo window in the kitchen, or it might be at the host desk—two key areas to control. So, this shift-floor manager (who is called a "babysitter or keyholder" in the industry) is there to provide coverage but not necessarily leadership.

Manager training is minimal, with most of it occurring on the job. The training basically consists of overlapping with other managers during their shifts and observing how things are done. Corporate restaurant chains' training programs for newly hired managers are more thorough. They need to be, because franchises and multiple outlets strive to have their locations run identically. Corporate-manager training programs have the manager trainees work every position. This includes the kitchen line, serving, and bartending. The importance of this type of training is both practical and emotional. In the event of a scheduling mishap, including a call off—or just the room being busy—the manager is trained to jump into a station and keep production flowing. Equally important, the manager gets to experience and hopefully empathize with the employees who are in these positions and what they must face day to day!

By training with an experienced store manager, the manager trainee will hopefully see as many day to day scenarios as possible and how they are handled. New corporate manager hires are also required to take tests and complete modules, to round out their training. They train in action-reaction behavior, which is how to deal with situations that a manager might encounter through the course of a day. This structural discipline is necessary because corporations and franchises want to take as much of the guesswork out of any decisions a manager might need to make. The action-reaction discipline relies on the practicing of "if this happens, you do that"—above all, making sure that the guest is satisfied in the event of an error or mistake.

Here's an example of the dynamic of how the manager is expected to behave. Let's say there's a customer at the table who's unhappy with how the food was prepared. The manager must do whatever it takes to ensure that the guest is content. Here, the restaurant could remake the dish that was prepared incorrectly and comp it—that is, take it off the bill. This can be done with one dish, a drink, or an entire tab. Free items usually help a guest to feel satisfied with an outcome, as long as the manager is respectful, sincere, and professional. Some concepts not only buy the meal but also give the guest an incentive to return, like a coupon or gift card. In the event of multiple problems at a table, managers are usually instructed to just comp the entire table. Guest perception is key. Yes, a mistake occurred, but it was handled appropriately.

One shortfall with this training is that it can miss situations where this approach fails to make the guest happy. Even though managers are mostly instructed to give away the house, when customers complain, sometimes the guest isn't content with just a comped item. Sometimes they are looking for an apology and validation that their concern was taken seriously. Businesses need to make sure their managers are properly trained and not risk the chance of a manager saying something wrong or having the guest feel insulted. In today's world, any negative word about a business can go viral on social media. The cost of putting out a fire, like when a customer feels there's been discrimination, for instance, is over a hundredfold the cost of comping an entrée or just saying "I'm sorry".

So, yes, I guess that anyone can be a restaurant manager if it means just holding the keys to the business and a code for the POS terminals. In my American government class in high school, when we were learning about constitutional laws and the lawyers who interpret them, I remember my teacher saying, "There are two types of lawyers: the ones who win and the ones who don't." She pointed out that all law-school graduates who pass the bar exam can fill out legal forms properly. They all know courtroom procedure and policy. But only a certain type of attorney wins—no secret there. And I am sure you can say that about any profession, including that of restaurant manager.

Some restaurant managers are better than others. But what makes them better? Is it their experience? Yes, that is a contributing factor. Other factors include temperament and the way they handle stress. But, again, the most important attribute is the manager's ability to communicate effectively with the customer as well as the staff. Unless managers can retain staff, keeping them engaged and motivated, the restaurant will not be successful. It will just be a business with a revolving door of employee turnover. Understanding how to get along with a diverse group of people and then integrating them into a healthy business culture are the manager's challenges. The manager must understand that his or her behavior influences the current culture. The business's culture will be positive if there is a real leader in place. It will be negative or toxic if there is an entitled boss driving the staff. So, what type of management team do you have in your business, and is it effective?

The responsibilities and expectations a manager must deal with daily are vast. The business's owners, including corporate ones, look for profitability. The numbers on profit-and-loss statements are the nuts and bolts on which the success of managers is evaluated. They must control costs. The snapshot of operations that the P&L provides is a useful tool for someone like an accountant who is measuring business efficiency. Do not underplay the importance of these numbers, because increasing the sales and profitability are what determines management success in the eyes of an owner.

## You Need a Business Model

You already know that the most important factor in creating a positive culture is the relationship between the management and the staff.

What does that mean? In today's society of too many cases of sexual harassment and discrimination, an open-door policy must be maintained to foster respect and trust between management and staff. What do managers expect from the staff, and what does the staff expect from management? The single most important thing on both sides is *respect*! This must characterize every conversation. The staff understands that the manager is a person of power. What the staff does not want to see is managers abusing their power to feed their own personal agendas. Personal agendas do not bode well for team environments. Why would the staff go the extra mile for a manager who wouldn't do the same for them?

These are some reasons that your management structure needs a model that represents the challenges a restaurant manager faces. These include working with a diverse group of people from many walks of life. Many employees in this business view their job with you as a stepping stone, while their primary goal might be to continue their education or because of the flexibility it allows. For the most part, because there are always exceptions, restaurants rely on young employees who are entering the workforce. In my own experience, I have hired many employees that have never held a job before.

Your model or system must be familiar to and understood by your staff. For any model to work and be successful, it must try to satisfy the wants and needs of employees at all positions. That is easier said than done, because different positions have different wants. The most obvious want is money. Money is a fundamental need that allows each of us to achieve our goals. But employees yearn for more than just money. They want to feel appreciated and valued by other employees and especially the management. They want to feel that they have a voice. For others, as I have witnessed, work gives a sense of self-worth and structure.

Respect seems to remain a constant need as we climb the totem pole. Another thing that employees need is to be recognized for going the extra mile. Acknowledging the employees who do a little extra goes a long way toward making them feel valued. For the part-timers on your staff, flexibility of scheduling is a definite need so that they can focus on their primary goals. For the career-minded managers, cooperation from the staff is a vital need. Teamwork is essential for success. All employees need an open line of communication with their superiors.

This model that I am referring to resembles a family. Take a typical management structure for a full-service restaurant and start at the top in regard to the faces of your operations—with the general manager. In this family model, the general manager is not the hard-core, military-drill-sergeant type who constantly barks orders. He or she needs a level of finesse and tact and is a parent figure—but can still look at the staff objectively.

To establish a positive culture, the general manager must be a pillar of stability, reasoning, authority, and, above all, fairness. He or she plays no favorites. The general manager sees everyone on the team as valuable. Unfortunately, most managers lack these abilities. The staff wants the managers to be consistent as far as temperament and behavior and to be approachable in the event of problems and disputes. Most important, they do not want to see any favoritism. The family model also works best in managing your staff due to the nature of the issues that it presents to you daily. I've already mentioned the melting pot of personalities and egos that must be managed, which is even more challenging when you must resolve conflicts.

Conflicts at your workplace are unavoidable, just as in any social setting. People will have different opinions and ideas. What a manager must be able to determine is if a conflict among staff members is the type that will escalate. Staff conflicts due to teammates not following policy or bending rules don't go away. The manager must not only be aware that a conflict exists but also deal with it swiftly and decisively.

Managers go through an evolution during their development. A manager's goal is not only to manage the team but to evolve into a leader. A leader knows the pulse of the staff. A leader is someone the staff trusts and someone who does not tolerate selfish behavior.

You have probably worked with some drama kings or queens before, maybe even currently. They create drama to serve their own interests. A small conflict might arise when one staff member approaches others to get a shift covered in a manipulative way. He or she plays on others' emotions to do this, maybe by trying to guilt them into saying yes. Another small conflict might be when staff members neglect duties, forcing others to cover them. While these may seem like small conflicts, if they are not handled well, they can lead to major issues. A manipulator should be looked at as a bully. He or she doesn't stop at the first no when manipulating, but persists and even shows anger at a refusal. There might even be crocodile tears. The slacker who lets duties go could be just lazy or entitled. When confronted about their performance, these types of people make excuses and skew the truth to justify their actions. The slacker is very quick to point fingers at other staff members with statements like, "I never see anyone else doing *X*," or, "I'm the only one that ever does *X*." Again, these situations might seem trivial, but they must be resolved quickly and effectively.

The general manager, if he or she is to be a real leader, has a great responsibility for maintaining a positive demeanor amid the chaos. The culture depends on it. The general manager also must bridge the managers of the front of the house and the back of the house. There can be no division, or an us-versus-them environment, between the front of the house and the back of the house. There is only one house, and everyone is part of the family. There can only be one team. There must be respect among the staff members when they communicate with each other. No condescension should be tolerated. Mentoring and training is required day in and day out. Managers must stay persistent in developing their teams, because there will be mistakes. There is a learning curve because you will find yourself hiring and training people in what may be their first jobs.

*In every business, in every industry, management does matter.*

Michael Eisner

Here is where management decisions affect the culture. Mistakes should not be penalized unless they are due to negligence. That should never be tolerated. If a mistake is made because an attempt at improving a current method didn't work well, there should be no punishment. A culture where employees fear making mistakes results only in your employees feeling nervous. A nervous employee never thinks of ways to improve procedures. All that a culture of fear does is discourage any form of creativity. What a shame. In my experience, some of the best operational changes have come from staff suggestions. Much of what I know today comes from making my own mistakes as well as observing and listening to the ideas of others.

## Optimal Interaction

Interaction with guests can occur when a manager performs a table visit or addresses a problem. Most customers like to have the manager stop by their table to ask about their dining experience. It adds that little touch of hospitality. Some establishments require a manager to stop by every table. This works fine when the restaurant is running smoothly, but this practice can be counterproductive otherwise. The manager ends up racing around, asking tables, "Howizeverything?" so quickly that it sounds like one word. When this added pressure is on your floor manager, who is also responsible for minute-to-minute operations, the guest perceives the manager as rushed and insincere.

Earlier, I mentioned that the servers must display hospitality and goodwill. The managers, hosts, bus personnel, and any other staff member who might interact with guests must do the same. Anyone on your team who has contact with a customer must think and act with a kind friendliness. The objective is to make sure that the guest is comfortable, relaxed and feels valued. This is why a positive culture is crucial. The goal is to have this behavior become second nature to staff members so that they *want* to give great service.

Ultimately it is your restaurant staff's hospitality that influences how your guest will feel. Having a manager zipping by a table and asking how the food is does not make guests feel comfortable. Sure, a manager touched that table, but they accomplished nothing in the way of building rapport and creating a return customer. In fact, for me, it is rather annoying to be interrupted in this way. Building rapport is one of the most important skills of salespeople. The customer must feel confident in your abilities and believe you. You must be genuine when making conversation with guests. If you can inject appropriate humor into your routine, you are on the road to building rapport. Other very important skills for putting a customer at ease are nonverbal. One to consider is the way you stand over guests. From the guest's perspective, you are looking down at them. Take a couple steps back. It will be more comfortable for both of you.

Other important practices for building rapport include eye contact and facial gestures. In the same way that a server may come across as aloof when reciting from a piece of paper, the blazing-fast manager comes across as very unnatural and insincere. What customers do take note of, however, is how the manager is helping or not helping the staff. I have a management philosophy that enables managers to interact with customers as they insert themselves into the flow of operation. I refer to this approach as "optimal interaction."

I noted that one of my earlier mentors used to say, "Control the controllables." The manager's function is to ensure the flow of business by keeping a finger on the pulse of operations all the while supporting the entire staff working in unison, like a machine.

Managers must be able to identify which part of the machine is becoming overloaded and where the pressure might run high. They need to be aware of which components of the machine might need help and which are about to burst. In short, the manager's job is to help staff members do theirs; the manager works for the staff. This point is so important! The manager's function is to ensure that staff members are successful by assisting wherever needed!

There are no special egos; there is only the team. Everyone is valuable. Success will not be achieved if the manager is not engaged in the flow of business. The efficiency of the restaurant machine hinges on the manager being involved. I view optimal interaction as a mind-set for the manager. It is a mind-set that wants to ensure that every team member, every component of the machine, is running efficiently. To create a positive culture of teamwork, the manager must be integrally involved. The team needs to feel that support, in case it's needed, is there. For the manager, the two most important areas to control are the host desk and the kitchen: the point of guest entry and the point of delivery of product.

First impressions are so important. A manager at the host desk has first contact with the guest before he or she is seated. This also identifies the manager as a person in charge, which could turn out to be important in the event of a problem at a table. The manager has already built some rapport and familiarity with the guest.

Another valuable opportunity for a manager at the host desk is to demonstrate correct behavior for the host staff. There is nothing better than that. This reinforces what they've been told to do by also showing them how to do it. For example, they will hear how proper greetings are made. The manager obviously cannot park at the host desk all night, but the control of the host area is important, because that is the first contact the guest has upon entering your place of business. Don't forget that guests choose to patronize your restaurant in order to eat. They expect to be acknowledged upon arrival and to be ushered to their tables promptly or be given an accurate wait time. They are hungry, especially if they have been waiting in line.

This takes us to probably the most important area of any restaurant: the kitchen, especially the area referred to as "the window," where the prepared food is detailed and garnished and where orders are assembled to be taken to the guest's table. This is what the game is all about—execution and delivery of product.

Now you might have gotten a chill, remembering some horrible experience at the expo window. The line cooks were stressed out because it was a rough, busy night; the servers were stressed out because they had to contend not only with the egos and attitudes of the cooks but also with a stressed-out customer. We had the expediter who lost control of the window and was ready to walk out the back door and go home in complete frustration.

Don't forget that for the most part, your staff members didn't sign up for chaos. As a manager, you must control the chaos. Managers cannot lose control. They must be pillars of stability. The culture depends on it! Managers must have the experience and knowledge to run the wheel of tickets and keep business flowing. They must also be able to jump in at the host desk and break the line at the door, all the while dealing with a table issue amid everything else. If you want to earn the respect of your staff, you must be able to lead it through the toughest of times. As a manager, if you can't see yourself handling those and similar scenarios day in and day out, turn and walk away now. No, turn and *run* away. This business is not for you.

Now, enough horror stories. Let's get back to a normal night when the restaurant machine is well oiled. The manager walks into the kitchen and helps deliver food. This not only allows the manager to touch the table, but it also enables him or her to make sure that the guests have everything that they ordered. Guests' perception is positive when they see a manager engaged in operations. When the flow of business is smooth, that is the time to stop by some tables to check on guests. If this feels intrusive, try stopping by to perform table maintenance. Pre-bussing is the easiest way to touch a table and spend a moment asking the guests how their food and dining experience are. Optimal interaction gets managers off the sidelines and puts them in the flow of operation.

For a truly positive culture, all managers must buy into the philosophy of teamwork. Managers set the pace for the staff, and they must lead by example. Another effect of optimal interaction is that when a manager interacts with a table, it creates positive energy. It enhances the experience for the guest. Do you know who also benefits from the enhancement of the guest's experience? The server. The manager just helped him or her to get a bigger tip. Better experience for the guest translates to a better tip for the server, which does wonders for morale. Optimal interaction raises staff morale while enhancing guest experience.

Are your managers capable of teaching their department staff how to perform their tasks? More important, can they get the staff to work as a team? Do they have the necessary attributes to deal with people? They'd better, because their employees are preparing and delivering the product to the customer. Managers must have the temperament to stay calm when mistakes happen, especially when things get busy. Managers also need to be fair and consistent in making decisions and not show favoritism. These qualities define your culture.

> *There are four ways, and only four ways, in which we have contact*
> *with the world. We are evaluated and classified by these four*
> *contacts: what we do, how we look, what we say, and how we say it.*

DALE CARNEGIE

Scheduling managers control the labor. They ensure that the operation maintains proper coverage during business hours. Here is where I differentiate between the front- and back-of-the-house staff. I refer to the front of the house as the sales floor and the back of the house as the production department. For the most part, the back of the house is staffed with more full-time employees than the front of the house. This means that the scheduling of the front of the house is more dynamic—there are many part-time people on the sales floor. The restaurant industry needs part-time people for certain positions so that it can accommodate peak-business times. These needs might be seasonal or weekly.

For example, weekend nights might be busy enough to need to double the staff on the sales floor compared to a slower, midweek day. This ebb and flow of scheduling needs is quite the challenge when it comes to staffing. A staff member assigned to the busiest nights of the week must be one of your best employees. You can't fill those positions with just anyone. He or she must have great product knowledge and also provide great service, or business will slide. So, here's the dilemma: you need part-time staff members to fill positions of peak business times. In order to attract and retain great employees, your organization must have a culture of respect for the individuals that show up for work every day and give their best. You must value your employees!

I've mentioned that part-time employees often have something that's a higher priority than their jobs. A flexible schedule that maximizes earnings ranks very highly in their decision to work with you. To retain the good employee, the scheduling manager must maintain a balance between allowing staff requests for flexibility and properly staffing the business. To accomplish this well, the manager needs to be firm but fair—which is easier said than done. I've noted that there is a melting pot of personalities on your staff, so maintaining a positive culture becomes even more challenging.

Being firm and fair is essential to maintaining a family model. The scheduling manager must be able to look at the business's needs objectively. Throughout this book, I have maintained the position of not playing favorites with the staff. However, there are exceptions which I would like to further explain. There is a difference between playing favorites and rewarding top performers. A common pitfall for a manager is playing favorites to a buddy. When preferential treatment is given to an employee because they appear to be a friend of the manager, this creates a negative moral amongst the staff. There might be some individuals on your staff who might go above and beyond expectations. Not only do these staff members perform their own duties, they also find time to help other staff members when they need it. This model employee, this "A" player, must be rewarded because they have earned it, and the team knows it. Here is where the parental model is important because it hinges on fairness all the while rewarding outstanding performance.

When confronted by the staff, a manager should acknowledge that this team member is being rewarded based on their willingness to go above and beyond to contribute to the success of the team as well as the business. The management should make it clear that all members will be rewarded if they also go above and beyond in support of the team. It's all about the team!

Outside of the busiest periods of your year, it is reasonable to accommodate employees' requests. Even during busy periods and holidays, there should be some sort of rotation among the staff. The manager should try to accommodate requests if possible, even if they are last minute. The way to do this is quite simple and logical: use rotation and reciprocation. If staff members see that the manager is trying to accommodate them, when the manager needs help covering a shift, the staff will try to help—and at some point, the manager will need that help.

When there is a level of respect between the management and the staff, they will work harder for each other. The scheduling manager has a challenging responsibility—even more so when there is a larger staff, with many of its members part time. The family model is also important for scheduling regarding events that affect the staff personally. All managers must empathize when employees have problems like child-care issues or personal-relationship issues that can affect someone's performance or ability to work. As a manager, you might find the staff coming to you seeking advice. The family model tends to have the greatest success here. You are ultimately a figure whom the employees see as empathetic to their struggles and want to see them succeed.

Your staff is your true asset; make them feel valued as such. Do not alienate them with indifference or rule with fear in any department, because those are not good for building employee morale. There is one area, however, where the parental model does not work for managers:

there must be a separation between work and leisure. Typically, a manager socializing outside of work with staff members, will lead to favoritism. As innocent as fraternization may seem, the staff will perceive the manager's lenience with some and not others. Your staff will also perceive this as a double standard or an unfair advantage towards the team members the manager socializes with.

The only time when fraternization between managers and subordinates is appropriate is during company events where everyone is included. Now, there is nothing wrong with your team hanging out together. It creates a camaraderie; however, your staff members should avoid dating each other. You can try establishing rules against it, but it is difficult to enforce. Your staff will do it anyway! And problems occur when relationships go through rough patches. It's inevitable. The problem then carries over into the workplace, and the whole staff will feel the tension. At some point, the employees involved in the relationship might not be able to work together any longer, and that's when things get tough for the business. It might lose one or both employees. When the dating involves a manager and a subordinate, however, things get a little more complicated. First off, as much as one would like to keep it a secret, that's impossible in a restaurant. The rumors will be running rampant. What started out as an innocent drink with the staff could not only turn into a nightmare for a manager, it could also turn into a nightmare for the business as well. Sexual Harassment. One acceptable outcome, for a manager dating a subordinate would be for one or the other to leave that store. Sexual harassment in the workplace is a discrimination that is affecting all industries. A study was conducted by ROC United and Forward Together who surveyed 688 current and former restaurant workers across 39 states. In their survey they found that two-thirds of the female employees and over half of the male employees claim they have been sexually harassed by a manager or supervisor. Further findings in their report cites that the Equal Employment Opportunity Commission (EEOC) finds the restaurant industry has the most sexual harassment claims out of all other industries. (ROC United, 2014).

In my experience, sexual harassment is not only evident in the manager-employee relationship. It also exists between co-workers and sadly enough with the customers too. Many times, sexual harassment is over-looked when the culprit is the customer. The servers or bartenders reasoning being, that's where their tip comes from, so they learn to deal with it.

Losing employees is something a restaurant must deal with. For most of your staff, employment with you is transitory—you are a stepping stone along the way to some other career. Yes, some veteran servers maintain part-time status to accommodate their lifestyle. The US Department of Labor found that the average of length employment for food-prep and service employees was just over two years in 2014, the same as it had been for at least a decade (US Department of Labor 2017). This is one of the lowest retention rates of any occupation. Being a manager, however, is a career choice.

Scheduling managers control the largest cost to a restaurant business: the labor. The other cost centers that must be controlled are food and beverages. Unless there is a retail cost center for things like merchandise, the kitchen and bar costs, along with labor control, determine the profitability of a restaurant or bar.

There might be areas in your business other than the major cost centers that must be managed. You might need an office manager, a catering manager, an events or marketing manager in addition to floor managers. Each one of your managers must have the traits for working within an established culture of teamwork and respect. The office manager, events manager, and maybe even the floor manager can be entry level, where minimal experience in restaurant operations is enough to get started. These jobs can be taught on the fly. That is not the case for managers who control the food and beverage departments. Experience is an absolute prerequisite for managing these departments.

A bar manager must have in-depth knowledge of bar operations and know how to tend bar. Just walking behind the bar rail when it is busy can be very intimidating. It is an extremely fast-paced and dynamic department. Your bar staff's responsibilities go beyond the scope of taking care of customers. Bartenders are responsible for the service bar, the area that provides beverage needs for the serving staff. In a typical server-banking scenario, the bartenders have the only cash register in the event that servers need change. If your establishment has any sort of state-run lottery, you guessed it—the bar team is responsible for that as well.

In most establishments, to advance to the bar team, someone is probably promoted from the server team. The bar staff must not only satisfy the needs of the bar customers but also the servers who are tending to the dining-room guests' beverage orders. A successful bar manager's most important skill is to deal effectively with the public and have the presence to lead and direct the staff. Having a presence, for any manager, is important if there is any chance of commanding respect from the staff. Without respect, there is very little willingness from the staff to follow orders and procedures.

A presence, however, can be either good or bad. Managers who control with fear have a presence that creates nervousness. This is a culture that restaurant businesses must avoid. You cannot afford to have an environment where the manager's personality creates fear. Such behavior reflects disrespect for the team, and you will lose quality employees.

The ideal bar manager must have basic math and organizational skills to either establish or follow par lists. Par lists are important for inventory control so you don't under- or overorder product. Organizational skills, like ordering from pars and even scheduling, can be easily taught to almost anyone. Those are the easy responsibilities. The manager must also have a keen eye and the experience to follow the operational flow from order taking through the ringing process.

The bar staff can get their own beverage product without needing to ring it in first. This allows for a wide range of dishonest behaviors.

Theft can happen at various levels—anything from not ringing in a drink order to overpouring a drink. Either way, the bar is losing money, so the bar manager must be able to spot it and deal with it effectively!

When you leave the front-of-the-house sales floor and enter the back of the house, you enter the production department. The chef or kitchen manager controls the food-cost center. The operation and managing of the kitchen is an incredibly difficult task. The chef's responsibilities range from the ordering and processing of product to its preparation and plating. Most every product that the chef or kitchen manager orders is perishable and has a short shelf life. Unlike that bottle of whiskey, which can sit on your liquor tier for months, fresh seafood lasts only days. The ideal candidate for chef must possess a level of passion—not only for creating dishes but for also developing a team that shares the same passion.

## The Road to Becoming a Leader

When creating a positive culture, department heads must be able to handle the power of being in control. Being in control means that you have a great burden of responsibility. This brings us back to the family model and the person at the top: the general or store manager. This individual is the bridge that interconnects every department within your business. Your team of managers must complement and have good chemistry with one another. Good chemistry is one of the most important qualities a team can have. The general manager must break down the walls, barriers, and egos that inhibit the management team from working as one. Power struggles create constant bickering, and a flow of negativity between managers must disappear if there is any hope of instilling a positive culture at your business.

Managers do control the business. However, they must do this by displaying confidence—and that is the ability to make good decisions that benefit the team. This is when the staff sees a manager as a leader.

What a morale booster it is when a manager makes a decision that benefits the team!

Control is a responsibility that is often abused. When managers feel the power that comes with control, their behavior can change. They can talk down to employees and can be closed-minded about ideas or suggestions from the team. The consequence of team members not feeling heard is that they start detaching—distancing themselves from the team—which then causes productivity to falter. The team's attitude becomes one of apathy. Once the staff begins to feel underappreciated or undervalued by the management, the culture rapidly declines. In such a case, the parental model fails due to the manager's changes in attitude and behavior. That is, the manager does not see the team as a family but as inferiors.

People try to give themselves the title of leader, but you can't give it to yourself. Your team gives it to you. "Leader" is a title you earn. A leader is something you evolve into; you are not born a leader. A leader has control of the environment, and if a manager does not, he or she will react incorrectly to situations. Leaders have learned through life and work experiences how it is best to respond. Rather than make quick decisions in the heat of the moment when emotions are running high, they refrain from decisions until matters have calmed.

Managers must remain calm and composed and not get emotional. Reactions based on emotion are perceived as aggressively irrational by the staff. A leader understands that business gets tough at times and that mistakes are going to happen. Leaders do not allow their emotions to get the best of them and start yelling at the staff. A leaders composure is also reflected in their body language. They do not get rattled and edgy. Leaders know to keep a positive demeanor during the chaos. That is important because the staff relies on it. When the stress of business runs high, the staff needs an individual to control the chaos, not fuel it. Employees feed off the demeanor of the manager when things get tough, so the manager needs to stay composed.

Great management is not easy. In my observations, managers will go through three phases of development: novice, adolescent, and leader. When a manager gets her or his first job managing a shift, he or she is just trying to figure out how to engage and be of some help. Unfamiliar environments can be overwhelming. The novice manager tends to stay quiet and reserved while trying to figure things out. The staff sees this individual as a key holder with minimal operational-management knowledge, and they are right about that. Furthermore, all restaurants are not run the same way. Each is unique, with its own flow of operation. Even for an experienced manager, there is a period of observation to learn the system that is in place.

What makes the restaurant or bar business difficult for a novice is that one cannot learn it from a class or a book. The restaurant business can only be learned in the field, through experience. The psychology of the restaurant machine can be mastered on one's own. However, it is easier when there is a mentor present—a leader. *Merriam-Webster* defines psychology as "the mental or behavioral characteristics of an individual or group." How a manager thinks and acts is the foundation for establishing a culture and continued success. Continued success for any manager in the food service, and probably the hospitality industry in general, is based on his or her ability to deal with people.

> *The ability to deal with people is as purchasable a*
> *commodity as sugar or coffee, and I will pay more for*
> *that ability than for any other under the sun.*

JOHN D. ROCKEFELLER

Once the novice manager starts showing signs of confidence and approachability, the staff will begin sharing all sorts of ideas with him or her. As they get more comfortable with the new manager, staff members will air their views about other employees and policies. This is an initial test of character for the new manager. As the staff trusts the new manager with different issues, the new manager must resist the temptation to voice any negative opinions about other staff members or policies. The manager's criticism will become gossip at blazing speed. This is one example of a pitfall that must be avoided because it will only contribute to the lowering of morale.

The parental model is used to deal with morale and many other situations. Say, for example, a parent has three children, each with strengths and weaknesses. The parents cannot show any signs of bias, because the children will immediately sense it. Furthermore, the other siblings will team up and harass the apparent favorite and be standoffish to the parents. Parents should never display favoritism. Parents must accept their children for their own abilities and individuality. Parental favoritism will only create alienation and self-esteem issues for children. The parental model applies the same mentality when it comes to managing the staff. Your staff members possess their own strengths and weaknesses, which a manager must be able to identify. Managers must avoid putting anyone in situations where they might fail. Employees are not created equal and putting one in a position of probable failure is a double negative. It not only gives struggling employees a complex that hurts their self-esteem but also creates a stressful situation for the staff who must pick up the slack.

After the initial adjustment to the new environment or position, a novice manager starts to feel comfortable in their role. They should be able to understand the business flow. And hopefully, by this time, they should know the best way in which to contribute to the team. Such contributions might be suggestions, such as on how to better perform or organize. This manager is entering phase two of development and is now the "adolescent." Suggested changes might be for operational improvements—showing a different technique for doing a side-work job quicker, for example. Did the manager think of it all on his or her own? Maybe. Or learn this technique somewhere else? More than likely. Again, you do not have to reinvent the wheel in this industry by coming up with new or revolutionary ideas. Any suggestion for being more efficient is welcome, even if it was copied from somewhere else. We all learn from someone or somewhere.

A manager's knowledge is a culmination of observations and working in different restaurant concepts with different people. This gives the new manager exposure to how other businesses operate within the restaurant industry. A manager's scope of vision and ideas is limited when they have only seen one business operate. Just patronizing other businesses does not give the knowledge needed for running operations but only a snapshot of product delivery. The true knowledge lies in working within that system. Experiencing day-to-day operations brings a behind-the-scenes understanding. The more exposure managers have to working within different systems, the more ideas and techniques they can implement at their current locations.

Excessive lateral moves for a manager, however, show that there is no stability in that applicant's longevity. For example, six to nine months at a location is not long enough to gain any insightful experience. Only with a significant length of exposure at a restaurant can a manager gain an insight on operations.

What happens in the adolescent phase of a manager's evolution is, unfortunately, unavoidable. It parallels what a parent might experience with teenagers, who go through a phase when they feel they know everything but really have only minimal knowledge. When managers in the adolescent phase implement a change, it gives them a feeling of being in charge, because only a boss can make a change. Managers feel like bosses because they possess power. The adolescent phase of managers' development is more self-serving and is steered toward fueling their egos. Their focus is all about their own advancement and betterment. Furthermore, when you are a boss and you give an order, employees must obey. Your management staff must able to enforce policy. If your staff is mostly composed of part-time, non-career-minded people, there must be checks and balances at your place of business. As a manager, you must expect a high level of accountability and professionalism from the staff.

Unfortunately, most managers never evolve out of the adolescent phase of management development, and there are a few reasons for this. One is that some managers cannot communicate effectively to their staff. They bark orders and make demands. A positive culture depends on staff members being respected and their opinions valued. When an order is given to a staff member, he or she must comply. When giving orders becomes excessive, the adolescent manager is heading down the road of micromanaging and absolute control. When this occurs, there is no room for staff members to think on their own. There is no taking possession of the situation and contributing on the staff members' part. Rather than include the staff in the solving of the problem, the manager disregards its opinions. The only time a leader should take full control and give direct orders is in the event of a crisis. Say the computer system goes down. This calls for a temporary solution. The leader gives direct orders on how to proceed with operations. Other than in emergencies, the staff must have a voice in resolving problems.

*Before you become a leader, success is all about you. When*
*you become a leader, success is all about growing others.*

JACK WELCH

Here is where the challenge lies for the person in charge. To make the transition to the final phase of development and become a leader, the manager must know that decision-making isn't about satisfying a manager's self-serving ego. It is about the success and continued development of the staff. The mentality of the evolving leader must be that the success of the staff comes first. Transitioning from phase two to phase three of the manager evolution and going from being a boss to a leader means putting the staff first. Where bosses think that the staff works for them, leaders feel that they work for the staff and strive to make sure they are successful. A leader is someone whom the staff trusts and respects. It could be the way that the leader starts the day by making initial rounds and greeting all team members. The manager should know each team member's name and even a little personal information. I know that some will disagree with me, but I believe that managers knowing a little of employees' lives outside of work shows that they care about them as people. Knowing a little personal information beyond name and job title goes a long way towards employee morale and productivity. A leader will know who on the staff is married, for example, and if they have children or what their goals or future plans might be. A leader understands that to form a bond of trust with the team, the team must be recognized as individuals. Only then will the team see the manager as approachable and feel comfortable coming to them with professional and personal issues.

A manager's success is based on the respect that they receive from the team. The more the staff respects the leadership, the better it will work within the established system. This is getting the most out of your employee, which is crucial for the success of a business like a restaurant. An easy way to gain respect from staff members is to show them respect first. A manager can do this by being sincere when congratulating or thanking a staff member. If a manager is not sincere, she or he is ultimately wasting everyone's time. Respect for the team is also shown when a manager engages and helps through optimal interaction. Respect also needs to be shown at the roundup or pre-shift meeting when the manager is speaking.

The pre-shift meeting is when the shift's employees gather and the manager reviews things like specials or events for the day, as well as any issues or policies that need mentioning. For the most part, posting notes or clock-in messages could relay that information, so this gathering of the team must be much more than that. This is when the staff is gathered without distractions. It's like a family gathering. If you have your pre-shift meeting in the kitchen, which you should, the cooks and dishwashers are also listening in. Sometimes the hosts and bussers are also listening, maybe just being curious and seeing what's going on. A manager might wonder what there is to talk about to what seems the same group of people every shift. Even if it is the same group, the goal is to keep everyone engaged in the meeting. This is your team. Acknowledge it as crucial to the success of the business.

This is also a sales meeting. Keep things positive and fun. Keep the energy high. Don't sink to the low level of finger-pointing or threats. That is futile, and all it does is create tension, which brings everyone down. Finger-pointing and laying blame bring no benefit. Here's what happens when a pre-shift meeting is negative. A server, a salesperson, is expected to go out in front of the customers and perform at a high level, after he or she was just subjected to fifteen minutes of bashing. Is this person going to have a smile on his or her face when talking to customers? A negative pre-shift meeting is not a great strategy if you want your sales team to provide great customer service.

Absolutely, there will be issues and other problems that must be addressed. Some things don't just go away on their own. How the manager addresses these problems is what dictates the work environment and culture. Are your managers communicating effectively? Are they talking down to the group, or are they really speaking to them? A manager must be able to connect with the staff. Your staff deserves to be treated with respect. Remember, if the staff believes in your ability and vision, its members will want to execute the directions they are given.

Getting the staff to believe in your ability to perform is the easy part. A manager displays competency by jumping in the trenches with the team, shoulder to shoulder, and helping. With most restaurant managers coming up through the ranks, they more than likely worked most positions, within the restaurant, and are familiar with what they need to do. Another important area the staff needs to see is your ability to handle stress. Managers must be able to control the chaos while controlling their tempers. A manager jumping in to help someone while obviously annoyed at having to do so doesn't go unnoticed by the staff.

The way management interacts with the staff defines the culture. Trust that everyone on the team watches how managers interact with other staff members. That manager's interaction with the employee sets the benchmark for acceptable behavior, which must hinge on respect. Positive interactions are what get a manager accepted by the staff as a hardworking, knowledgeable manager who cares about its success. That is a crucial step to start being identified as a leader. Being perceived as a leader gives one a higher status than just being a boss. One day I overheard a conversation between a few servers saying how I was such a great team player. One server jumped in and said that I wasn't just a team player; I was the coach.

An intimidating manager or boss gets employees to do things, because there are consequences attached to not following orders. The do-this-or-else approach causes fear and resentment in employees, because the consequences could affect their pocketbooks and livelihoods. A leader takes a different approach. Leaders can get better results from the workforce, because they continuously lift and develop the staff. Constantly developing the staff is a prime indicator of an individual who chooses to put the staff first—sometimes even before the guest. This individual is a leader.

Let's say a manager delivers a directive to the team on changing the way something is done. The manager tells the staff what to do, and it's the staff's job to do it. Here's the challenge—how do you get staff to want to do it because it believes in your judgment and vision? How can you encourage your staff to comply? You are not a personal trainer at a gym who stands behind the staff, pushing them to finish reps: "Come on, only three more reps. Let's go, you can do it." You will hear the word "motivator" thrown around. "He really knows how to motivate the group," they say. As you speak to your team, you are trying to get everyone all fired up. It is a sales meeting, after all. You want to get everyone focused and excited to go out and face the public.

The meeting ends, and the staff hits the floor. But as time passes, the message becomes only a memory. You hope the staff remembers it. You need to inspire your staff so that they want to follow the directive. When you implement a change, you can feel the level of your staff's anxiety rise. The difficulty of the change or adjustment determines the level of stress. It is important to support your staff members during transition, because they might become edgy and nervous. This can affect the productivity of veteran staff, because they already have familiar ways of working. Change is easier with newer hires, because they aren't set in their ways yet.

In a college engineering course, my professor mentioned something that just stuck with me. The topic was the flow of electricity and the way that current moves through various loads. I will not bore you with any formulas, but the message was that electricity takes the path of least resistance, which is the one with the smaller load. I see a parallel here with how we deal with most obstacles. Employees also look for the path of least resistance and the easiest way to accomplish tasks. They cut corners. This does not necessarily imply laziness. I am just saying that people are more comfortable performing tasks they are familiar with. The more familiar they are with the task, the more inclined they are to look for easier ways to complete.

The problem with getting comfortable at performing tasks is the risk of becoming complacent—being satisfied with how things are, and not trying to make them better. This is when a manager who tries to implement a change to make things better, will run into resistance. Complacency works against any attempt at a change and is a terrible attitude for an employee to have. A comfort zone, on the other hand is, as *Merriam-Webster* defines it, "the level at which a person functions with ease and familiarity." People learn how to keep up with the demands of business flow. They are naturally creatures of habit and are afraid of the unknown. They establish their systems or routines and are reluctant to try anything that veers from the familiar. When the culture depends on staff adhering to a change, it is imperative that it does not fall back into a comfort zone when things get busy and stressed.

*When you make a mistake, there are only three things you should
ever do about it: admit it, learn from it, and don't repeat it.*

PAUL BEAR BRYANT

Fear of failing is one of the reasons that people are afraid of change. This is where a leader can ease the transition of change, because failure or mistakes are part of the growing process. We all make mistakes; however, we need to learn what we did wrong. What a manager does not want to see is repeated mistakes. When managers see that, they must make sure that their directives are crystal clear. In my experience, when employees repeat a mistake, they either don't understand the directive or choose not to follow it. If they are struggling to grasp information, the manager must decide how much more time and energy to spend on that employee's training for that position. Some people might not be able to perform at the level requested. If the employee has simply chosen not to follow the directives, that is their choice—but it is the manager's choice on how long they wish to tolerate that behavior. I choose to quickly address problems with employees not following directions, because these individuals are working against the culture. That is unacceptable. Unless the manager can get to the root of the problem and rectify it, the employee who chooses not to adhere to the change must go. It's unfortunate but necessary.

So, where do you find a restaurant manager? Do you need a shift manager or a store-level manager? Regardless, the candidate must be able to work within the parental model as well as understand the importance of a culture that is built on teamwork and respect. Recruiting is time-consuming and costly. Start by posting the job online. You'll have dozens of applicants within days, but there is still plenty of work to do in filtering through the applications. Another recruiting option can be to spread the word through your vendors. A sales rep makes many stops like yours and talks to a lot of people in the industry; he or she could help recruit by putting out feelers. Sometimes the greatest referrals come from the most unexpected sources. You can also use headhunters, but that is the costliest way to recruit. One benefit of using a recruiter is they will sift through all the applicants and only set interviews with qualified candidates.

How about promoting a diamond in the rough among one of your current employees? Well, how can you tell if he or she has leadership potential? Any candidate would have to show that they can carry their weight and contribute to the business's success by excelling in their respective areas. Another indicator is a willingness to help other staff members when they see things done incorrectly or not to standards. That is a key cog for the restaurant machine to be successful. As I've been saying, the culture is the way people behave when no one is watching.

Yes, successful restaurant managers are developed in the field; however, some additional good qualities are sometimes taken for granted. Management candidates should show up for work every shift, on time, and bring their best game. They don't play around while on the clock but keep themselves busy and useful. You would like to think that all your employees are like that, but the reality is that they are not. What you do know, however, is what characteristics and work ethic you have in your employee. You know this candidate's strengths and weaknesses, along with what type of person they are.

Another reality, which was mentioned earlier, is that not all employees are created equal with respect to skill level. Some employees can work magic controlling their areas of responsibility and make their job look effortless. There are cooks who can run the entire line by themselves while still producing a great product. The truth is, though, that just because someone is a great cook or bartender doesn't mean that he or she will make a successful manager. There's much more to it than just being great at a position. A manager's greatest skill is the ability to deal with people and communicate effectively.

If your business is looking for a cog to insert to keep the current system in place, promoting from within might make the most sense. This is a candidate who already understands the current system and has had success working within it. But it is a different ball game to manage people. One of the major hurdles for the promoted employee is managing former coworkers. This has nothing to do with skill level but with being acknowledged and taken seriously in the new role. For businesses with multiple locations, it might be beneficial to transfer the manager candidate out to another store for training and placement. This makes the transition much easier.

Another perspective for consideration is that an employee who has worked for many years on the floor or in the kitchen might naturally be ready for advancement to manager. Here is a common scenario that I have observed over the years for long-term industry employees. When they first stepped into a restaurant or bar in their teens, it was probably their first job—such as a bus-person, host or dishwasher. As time passed, the employee advanced to serving or cooking. With the naturally high turnover rate in the restaurant business, it is not that difficult for a hardworking employee to get a chance and get promoted. If the employee continues to be dedicated and work hard, he or she might even run that store one day, climbing all the way up the ladder

However, the restaurant or bar business does have some pitfalls for career employees that cannot be sugarcoated, especially for a person raising a family. The hours are long and sometimes unpredictable. It's a given that you must work weekends and holidays. And then there are the late nights in the bar industry. These pitfalls might be acceptable for a single employee, but for married employees with children, it becomes a little more challenging than a traditional nine-to-five job. Everyone needs to find a work-life balance to have any longevity in this business.

When I interview, I rely on my intuition. As an interviewer, you must know what the position is and what it entails; preferably, you have worked it before. How can you hire for a position without knowing all its responsibilities? Then, what is your first impression of whether this person can do the job and work within the established culture? Your gut feeling takes you beyond the résumé and to the person sitting across from you. What the résumé doesn't tell you is if the candidate can get along with the other managers and the staff. Fitting into the desired culture is essential and being respectful of fellow staff members is an absolute requirement. If your gut feeling is that this candidate cannot handle the demands of the position or work within the culture, move on to the next candidate.

I cannot stress the importance of selecting people with the right personality and temperament. Many things can be taught, but being nice and working with others, unfortunately, is difficult to teach, if it can be taught at all. It's like trying to change someone's personality.

Hiring employees is not easy. If you are still not sure of the candidate and want reassurance on his or her character, you must look beyond references. No one lists references who give negative reviews. To find out about potential candidates, you must go to their previous or current employer and ask their peers about them. You must be discreet and tactful in your approach, but you will get a more honest reference—which may be good or not so good. A question to ask the candidate's peer would be, "What do you like about so-and-so?" An answer such as, "He's all right," or, "She's OK," may mean that the person is perceived as mediocre. Peers should sing praises for their teammates. Don't ask questions that might be construed as negative or overly inquisitive. The candidate's peers may become apprehensive. They will not talk negatively about their peers or managers; they just met you. The facial expressions a person makes, however, speak volumes in addition to the words they might say.

You get better at interviewing with experience and thus are better able to follow your instincts. After your gut feeling tells you that you have an acceptable candidate who can work within your system and culture, look at the résumé. First, is the candidate's experience in line with the position offered? Is he or she underqualified, overqualified, or just right? This information has to do with compensation. If employees are undercompensated by industry standards for their experience, they will feel undervalued, and that may lead to underperformance. The candidate may initially accept the position, if offered. However, under compensation and seeing no room for growth will keep them active in their job search. Everyone needs an income.

Second, I look at the time spent at previous employers. It gives a great indication of the candidate's level of commitment. Hiring managers do not want to see a lot of job hopping in a short period. Unfortunately, there is no way to gauge these attributes when you hire someone from a job posting. You know nothing about the individual's work ethic or people skills. People put their best foot forward in interviews, but it usually takes about a month of working with them before you start seeing their true selves.

When managers feel that they have hit the ceiling within their current organization, they seek out opportunities for growth. Restaurant and bar managers, like everyone else, want to maximize earnings and career-advancement opportunities. Your new manager could be fairly new to the industry or a seasoned veteran.

You will train all new hires to learn your system, including opening and closing procedures, basic responsibilities for running a shift, and, eventually, ordering and scheduling. That's what textbook training gives you. Here's what textbook training doesn't give you. It can't give you the type of lesson and exposure that life experience will. Let's back up and start at the interview process.

For whatever reason, the candidate felt the need to move on from his or her previous employer and probably managed at another operation. Being selected from a pool of applicants is a tremendous ego boost for anyone. The person jumps in and starts learning and becoming familiar with the operational flow and the staff. Chances are that the new job is similar to the previous one since it is still in the restaurant industry. That's the easy part. New managers notice how the new team is working and interacting—they are sensing the culture, whether they know it or not. They gather information on how things really work.

There is no cookie-cutter approach to managing restaurants, because every business is unique. The vision, identity, and system are put in place by the owner, and new managers must fit into the current chemistry. They must have positive interaction with everyone, especially the staff members whom the upper management or ownership hold in high regard. This is restaurant politics. These staff members could be anyone from the accountant to the executive chef. Sure, new hires might have soared through the interview process on impressive credentials. Once training begins, however, they are at ground zero once again—they have to gain team respect and show their competency. New managers must resist the urge to initially change the way things are done.

Another downside is that new managers don't know what the involvement of the ownership is until they have been working for a while. There are many types of owners out there. Some absentee owners empower their managers to run the business and hold them accountable for profitability. Other owners are very hands-on and are on site almost every day during peak business hours. Then there are the owners who want to run the business from the sidelines. This is the most challenging type to work for. Owners should be hands-off unless they are involved in the day-to-day operations. Owners who are approachable and open to suggestions understand that the restaurant world is evolving and change is constant. All owners should have an eye on the industry and be aware of what the competition is doing.

Culture starts at the top with the ownership. How do the owners look at the people working for them? Owners cannot rule with an iron fist and not show gratitude toward their employees. The true assets of restaurants are not the brick-and-mortar buildings or their ownership. The true assets of any hospitality business are the employees who show up for work every day and give their best effort. The true assets are the staff, and they must be treated fairly and with respect.

When a business's culture or environment is on the decline, the reason is not always easily identifiable. There are many factors that could be responsible. For one, the ownership could be faced with the reality that the way things have always been done isn't working effectively anymore. The frustrating part is, they can't put their finger on why it is happening. The owners might have invested a considerable amount of money into renovating the establishment, revamping the menu, and increasing their marketing budget, all to no avail. This is when the ownership starts to pressure the management. The owner will point out customer-service complaints rearing their ugly heads on social media and the climbing employee-turnover rate. A high employee-turnover rate, in my opinion, is an important indicator of the culture. Retaining employees is crucial to success.

I am talking not about employees leaving for career advancement but about those leaving because they are not happy. Unhappiness can be due to low pay, but it's usually because of a negative environment—one where the employees don't feel they have a good working relationship with the manager. A toxic culture drives good employees out.

When a store-level manager feels pressure from the upper ranks for store performance, a weak manager will have difficulty accepting any of the blame or responsibility. He or she concludes that everyone else on the team is doing things wrong. This is where the blame game starts and blame runs downhill in an organization. It becomes very difficult for the store level manager to face the reality that control is being lost. Rather than accepting responsibility, a weak store manager will enter preservation mode and start pointing fingers at assistant managers and department heads. This reaction is due to the store manager's inability to identify the root problem but nonetheless is being pressured to act. He or she continues as before, but at a feverish pace, like the driver of a car that is stuck in the mud—the driver keeps stepping on the gas, causing the tire to sink lower and lower, ultimately making things worse. This gradual loss of control can be attributed to a combination of complacency on the store manager's part and a lack of understanding on how to deal with people and their personalities.

Many times, the road to store manager is through climbing the ranks. Many successful managers have taken that route as I explained earlier. They probably started in the business as dishwashers or hosts. The dishwasher might become a cook and the host a server. This system is valuable because the experience and exposure are important. They give an appreciation of those entry-level positions. The exposure to working various positions gives a better understanding of what I refer to as the restaurant machine. One must walk a mile in someone else's shoes to understand what his or her position entails. The exposure should also lead to an appreciation for the importance and necessity of all departments working in harmony for success.

As time moves forward, so does that dedicated employee's advancement to manager. She or he already knows the business at that location after being there for years. Now this manager is running shifts and will eventually control cost centers.

The restaurant world is very dynamic as far as employee turnover is concerned. This holds true for managers as well. The manager who comes up through the ranks could possibly be the store manager one day. There probably is no other person in the building who has a better understanding of the ins and outs of the business's flow and cycles. Am I describing the perfect employee? Well, there might be a flaw if this manager has not learned how to deal with people. If this manager's actions are based on knowledge acquired by witnessing other managers responding to similar situations, you hope the influencer's style was one of respect and valued the team. A person's management style is simply a combination of lessons learned and their personality.

It is very important for a manager's reaction to situations to be controlled and calm. This is important, because you must have a basic understanding of how people think and react. All managers should constantly try to get better at understanding the human psyche. *Merriam-Webster* defines *psyche* as "the soul, mind, or personality of a person or group." Personality theory, however, can be very complicated and confusing. There are so many theories on how the psyche works. Here, I am only going to give my interpretation of *how* people react to various stimuli without trying to explain *why*. I also use "personality" and "ego" interchangeably here.

Let's say an employee is making mistakes during a busy shift. A manager could decide not to react at all to the situation, to avoid confrontation. If the staff sees the manager avoid the employee and act as if nothing is out of the ordinary, hoping the problem will go away, the staff will think the manager is spineless. What about the manager who yells? Yelling is not an appropriate reaction to any situation unless you are a Navy Seal drill instructor. Yelling at employees just drives them away and alarms the rest of the staff witnessing the outburst.

The staff relies on the manager to remain calm when the stress of the business runs high. A manager who yells will be seen as unstable, and that will only cause fear among the team and have them walking on eggshells. Yes, you will get everyone's attention when you yell but you will also lose their respect. This also applies to the staff. The desired culture does not tolerate team members yelling at each other. In the event of a disagreement, the dialogue will be in a calm tone and be respectful. The right managerial personality can identify mistakes and go right to the side of the server to help. If the server is completely overwhelmed, the manager will delegate help. The right type of ego would know that this is the time to focus on the most important matter. If the server is struggling and making mistakes, it can only affect customer service negatively. The manager's only priority at that moment should be guests who might be suffering from lack of service. You need the person whom you call your manager to have the correct temperament and to understand that any discussion of how or why things went astray can wait. Egos are fragile.

A store manager who is faced with ownership bringing in another experienced manager goes into self-preservation mode and tries to protect his or her position. When an ego feels threatened, it will naturally try to defend itself, to try to survive. One defense mechanism we have all probably used, to cover up or ease the pain of a threat, is denial. A manager may not acknowledge there is a conflict or problem at all.

The initial reaction from the store-level manager, in the case of a veteran new hire, is to protect his or her position and the current system, which is what he or she knows and understands. In the eyes of the store manager, any suggestions of change are a threat. Change takes people out of their comfort zones—which, again, leads people to keep doing things the way they've always been done. We are creatures of habit. Here's the difficult problem: this shortsightedness that questions change is usually the main obstacle to an organization's advancement.

This is where denial masks that a problem exists. Unless the manager can identify that there is a problem, he or she cannot put pride aside and admit that a change is necessary to a policy or procedure that he or she probably established. This resistance to change brings a negative energy to all the staff. In trying to establish a culture of teamwork and respect for one another, negativity at any level becomes poison. Any tug-of-war of egos and pride among the management only feeds the poison. One challenge with change is being able to explain why it is necessary.

There will come a point when a veteran-manager new hire might feel more experienced than their supervisor in many areas, such as in expediting the delivery of product or restructuring policies and procedures. The dilemma is that the store manager will resist the changes that the new hire suggests. Here is where personality influences behavior, and the veteran-manager new hire needs to control his or her ego even when he or she knows more than the current manager and could do a better job running the show.

If you find controlling your ego difficult, just remember that you applied for the position. If you find yourself that frustrated and unhappy, realize that no one is forcing you to stay. Your responsibility is to do the job that you were hired to do, to the best of your ability. It's why you are paid. Maybe the reason you were hired was the exposure and experience you do have in the industry. Rather than being combative and badmouthing the supervisor's ideas, the veteran hire should use his or her experience and help restructure business plans. Above all else, never insinuate to your upper manager that you are smarter. Regardless of whether upper management likes your ideas, their egos may not allow them to implement them if they are made to feel ignorant or inferior. New manager hires must stay humble when they make suggestions. This could possibly turn into an opportunity to move up in an organization, especially if there are expansion plans in the works for the company. Just remember to always have the best interest of the business in mind with what you say and what you do.

A weak store manager will take the job-security approach. This mentality is so frustrating to the rest of the staff, including other managers. The store-level manager in this mode won't delegate daily decisions and also keeps cost control to himself or herself. This manager believes that by controlling the important responsibilities, he or she is indispensable. This further separates the manager from the staff, because it is a "boss" mentality.

True success for a store manager comes from the ability to assemble a team of managers and staff that believes in the company's direction—a true leader. Store managers don't have to be the best at every position. They just need to be great at delegating responsibility. Where the store manager must be great is in dealing with people and bridging departments to work together.

There is a special approach to managing people more experienced than you. When you are dealing with new-to-the-industry hires, you need the ability to train, teach, and develop them. When you are dealing with an experienced, successful chef, however, the approach is very different. Every person must be treated and spoken to with respect. That is a given for any chance of establishing a positive culture. Where managers fail in bridging departments is their inability to communicate effectively. How can a front-of-the-house manager with little-to-no kitchen experience tell this chef what to do and how to do it? This is how tension is created among your management team.

If you do not include the chef in the upper ranks of management, you are really missing the big picture. I am not talking of a kitchen manager at a corporate chain, who also has important responsibilities. I am talking of an individual who creates food dishes, a chef who controls the ordering of food as well as the labor in the back of the house. The kitchen team is where the greatest percentage of money is invested. So instead of approaching the chef and saying, "I want you to...," try a different approach. Ask for the person's input and help in coming up with a solution. Remember that there are two ways to speak to someone. Do not come off as a condescending boss. Any employee will be more willing to help if he or she is included in the decision-making process.

A true leader can inspire the staff, including managers, to be better. The management is the most important cog in the restaurant machine for establishing a positive culture. Management now has an incredible responsibility—to assemble and develop a staff. It is the staff that has direct contact with every guest that enters and exits your place of business. As much as the managers preach policies and procedures, it is the staff that must follow through and execute on them.

## SECTION III

# It's All About the Team

● ● ●

MANAGERS ARE FACED WITH THE difficult task of staffing the business. Recruiting your staff, your hourlies, is not much different from recruiting a manager. It is all about finding the right people with the right personalities. But one difference when recruiting staff members for various positions is that you will be interviewing people with limited experience and availability. Prospects could range from current students to parents and maybe to some people looking for a second job. These candidates usually pick up part-time jobs to generate some cash flow.

> *The US Bureau of Labor Statistics says that In the United States,*
> *there were over 2.2 million combined food-preparation and serving*
> *workers in 2016, with more than half of them being part time.*

Some positions in restaurants are entry level and require no experience. Training and development occurs on the fly. With an on-the-job training approach, the screening of hires becomes that much more important. Certain personality types do better serving, and others do better with back-of-the-house responsibilities.

If you deal with people as your occupation, you must have a basic understanding of the human psyche and personality types, and interviewers need this too. According to Carl Jung, people are generally either introverts or extroverts. *Encyclopedia Britannica* says of Jung's categories:

An introvert is a person whose interest is generally directed inward toward his own feelings and thoughts, in contrast to an extravert, whose attention is directed toward other people and the outside world. The typical introvert is shy, contemplative, and reserved and tends to have difficulty adjusting to social situations. The extrovert, by contrast, is characterized by outgoingness, responsiveness to other persons, activity, aggressiveness, and the ability to make quick decisions.

This typology is now regarded as overly simplistic because almost no one can be accurately described as wholly introvert or extrovert. Most persons fall somewhere between Jung's two types—i.e., they are ambiverts, in whom introversive and extroversive tendencies exist in a rough balance and are manifested at different times in response to different situations.

Even the most introverted of your new hires applied for work and engaged in some communication. You already know that interviewees put their best feet forward and try to make great first impressions and that the interviewer must look beyond the facade and talk with prospects. Don't bother asking how they would handle various situations; you will teach them your policies and procedures for that. But how do prospects respond to questions? Do they use one-word responses, or do they answer in more depth? Are they looking you in the eyes or down and away?

It is important to learn how to pick up on psychological cues, because you must have the correct people in the correct positions. A leader must have a basic understanding of personality types, because it is important to know how an employee might react in various situations. A leader will not put team members too far out of their comfort zones, where they are likely to not be able to carry their weight. This is one example of a workplace stressor where the team is expected to pick up the slack. Controlling as many stressors in the workplace as possible will not only help in creating a healthy work environment, it is a necessary component to creating a positive culture.

Of course, there really is no way to know how any person will respond in any given situation. How can you possibly predict that in an interview? The hiring manager must take their first impression of the candidate and use their experience and intuition to choose the best available applicant. This is true for servers and bartenders as well. One thing to keep in mind is that you will not truly know the work ethic of your employees until they become acclimated and comfortable in their new environment. You can more easily train employees on the point-of-sale system than on being nice and working well with others.

Let's look at the customer's first impression of your business: the host. For this, you are looking first and foremost for a ready smile when greeting guests. There should be a natural pleasantness about hosts even when they are just standing there. Another important skill is the ability to stay calm under pressure.

Keep in mind, though, that you can't assume that a quiet, reserved individual will not do well in a particular position. Take another example, like that of a server in the front of the house. She or he might seem introverted but could be very detail oriented and responsive to guests' needs. Conversely, a person who seems outgoing might fold under stress or social pressure. This is where hiring managers must go with their gut instinct, which relies on their experience and understanding of people.

Dishwashers and bus personnel, on the other hand, require self-motivation. Most of your employees have responsibilities that require them to keep up with the demands of business flow. Your hosts, for example, must immediately greet the guests and get them into seats. Your servers and bartenders immediately respond to the newly seated guests. The order is sent to the kitchen, and your kitchen team prepares the fare. Positions that are not directly involved in the minute-to-minute operation of serving the guest must be able to keep themselves active. The bussers need to keep busy when there are no dirty tables, and it's the same for dishwashers while they are waiting for dishes. Too much of an outgoing personality at these positions might lead to an awful lot of talking. And when there is too much talking, neglecting duties and productivity become compromised.

When staffing for the restaurant, you are trying to gauge work ethic and attitude from the pool of candidates. Personality and mannerisms do not weigh as heavily for back-of-the-house employees as they do for the front of the house, like a server. Members of the back of the house, the kitchen team, rarely interact with the guest. When staffing a restaurant, first impressions and gut instincts are very important. Sure, you can look at a résumé and ask questions about how prospects would do this and that. Those textbook questions and answers are pointless, because they give no true insight as to how someone will behave in a given situation.

Veteran candidates can give you the textbook response to most of your questions and scenarios. This does not mean they can follow through with them, though. Veteran candidates can tell interviewers what they want to hear. You must talk with candidates until you are confident about their abilities. If you are familiar with the position offered, you can sense if the candidate might work out. For example, was it your first impression that your chef candidate had leadership ability and would be able to maintain control in this position? You want the posture of an individual who will lead your kitchen to be alert and firm. You don't want the person's leadership style to be loose and sloppy. You want chef candidates to show passion when they are talking about dishes they've created and to convey that passion to the rest of the kitchen staff.

Your gut feelings are rarely wrong if you know what characteristics are required for a role. You need to feel that the candidate also has a knack for organization and numbers, because chefs control the back-of-the-house labor and ordering of food products, which are the greatest costs to your business. The position of chef is not one for clock watchers. The chef must be fully committed and be able to lead during peak business hours. The chef is there until the job gets done.

Having the right people at the right positions is crucial to success. That is why it is so important not to separate the front and back of the house. The leader is expected to bridge these areas. A leader understands, however, that to effectively run an operation, there must be key individuals at all positions to help maintain standards. These individuals include the chef, other managers and even team members. No person can do it alone. With so many employees needed to serve a guest, the established culture of the restaurant must be one of teamwork and camaraderie. This becomes crucial in the goal to exceed guests' expectations.

A simple definition of culture is that it's the way that people are taught to behave in society. And your society is your staff. You show your staff what needs to be done and how to do it. Then you expect its members to do it the way that you showed them. If a manager's job was only that easy! Changing or establishing a culture starts with the management team, which is involved in the day-to-day operations. Restaurants are not businesses you can lead from the sidelines. True leaders are accessible to the staff when they need them the most—when the restaurant is busy or during peak hours.

Just being accessible, however, is not enough. A leader must stay engaged in the operations. That is why optimal interaction is so successful. The manager patrols the room and assists the staff and the guests. A leader's actions and behavior are adopted by the staff. The way that managers communicates with the staff shows the level of respect that managers have for them. A great way to gain respect from the staff, for starters, is to acknowledge your staff as vital members of the team. Great teams are born when staff members help, challenge, and develop each other to improve. The success of any new hire rests with your veteran team helping in his or her development. When your staff is doing the right things when no one is watching, you have established a positive culture.

It is time to either recruit your team or further develop who you have. The building of a winning team is where the difficulty lies. There are so many personalities to contend with. Managers have the difficult task of evaluating the staff individually. They must be objective and focus on the strengths and weaknesses of each team member. Managers must ask themselves objectively if the business is a better place with or without each individual. Managers, to be successful, must maintain a team chemistry—members that complement each other.

When expectations are being communicated, they must be crystal clear. The staff needs to know the big picture; for the front of the house, the job is selling service, and for the back of the house, it's producing a consistently great product. Yes, the front of the house sells service. It might deliver the products that the kitchen prepares, but ultimately, it sells the guest an experience through service.

You also want to have an environment where your staff is interacting in a fun manner, as long as the primary focus is providing a great dining experience for the guest. Keep the fun on the sales floor and not in the kitchen or side stations. Furthermore, fun can only be achieved when the restaurant machine is running well. One problem that is common in the restaurant business is fatigue. There might be days when it is so busy that there is no time for a break. I am not referring to a busy dinner rush. I am referring to being lined-up all day and flipping table after table, hour after hour. Fatigue will set in. An employee, like a server for example cannot leave their section unattended for a break without someone covering. Who would be tending to the customer? When employees start getting fatigued, mistakes will happen. It is the responsibility of the manager to make sure the atmosphere stays positive and that the guest does not feel the stress that the employees may be experiencing.

It is no secret that there is no long-term vision for most employees who make a job of restaurant work. The realization is, your employees show up for work because they have bills to pay and want cash in their pockets. It's fine if the motivator for employment is money. We all need to get paid. Remember, though, it is your culture that keeps employees. Some people select a career in the restaurant business, as I did. If the business is in your blood, there are not many other environments that offer such a high-energy, socially interactive setting. The restaurant and bar business can be fun with the right culture in place.

With the restaurant industry having such a high turnover rate, it allows lateral moves for employees between restaurants and bars to be relatively easy. An employee can leave your restaurant or bar to work for your competition. There is no bigger regret for a manager than to lose a good, quality employee to the competition.

## Is Your Work Environment Toxic?

An employee might leave for other reasons beside money and new opportunity. The restaurant business, particularly serving, is a great way to make some extra cash for people with a need for flexibility. Regarding the quick turnover of employees, some might last only six months to a year. It's very transitionary at times. It is also very costly, because it takes someone a couple months to become proficient and adjust to your business flow and culture. In many cases, that's just the nature of the business. However, when you lose employees because of the work environment, that is a sure sign that the culture is toxic.

Toxic work environments are easy to identify in restaurants. The staff is visibly angry. That is a big red flag indicating the overall morale. There will be a lot of frustration and arguments between staff members. Managers often show favoritism, and there is an overall lack of respect among the staff. Managers tend to look the other way when they witness arguments or problems, especially if the favorite is involved. Basically, it is an out-of-control environment with the staff running the show. It becomes a free-for-all when things get a little busy. Many managers fail here because they are unable to identify the root of the problem—so they can't come up with a solution. In my experience, a toxic work environment doesn't happen on its own. It is caused by a combination of toxic employees and the management's inability to control.

If you want to establish a positive culture, you must take an objective look at the staff. After the management, the staff is the next most important component in creating a positive culture. A manager can only hope to have a team of A players, where he or she expresses the goals and expectations and the staff overdelivers. The reality is, some employees will fail to adapt to change. You will give these employees time to adjust and prove themselves, but they may still fail. Some employee types contribute to the toxicity of the environment. Let's see how they can affect the general morale.

*A-plus players like to work together and they*
*don't like it if you tolerate B work.*

STEVE JOBS

First, I'll discuss the "slackers." We have all seen them. They're never around when help is needed, like at a busy expo window. In side work, they only do the bare minimum. Again, a culture is how your employees behave when no one is watching. Slackers take no initiative or ownership of anything. They are not truly part of the team. Slackers' behavior upsets your A players. It also creates frustration when the behavior is tolerated. At first, your A players will just complain, but if the manager does not act on the complaint, it compounds their frustration. When A players stop complaining, it is a sign that they are starting not to care. Often, this is the time when they begin searching for employment elsewhere. When employees don't care about the business, it is a disaster. You can't establish a positive culture or be successful.

Now let's discuss the "weak links." Occasionally a person is hired or promoted who might have been good at a previous position but finds that the current level of stress is greater and that better organizational skills may be needed. The weak link is making an effort but simply can't handle the job. There is no easy position in a restaurant when things get busy. Regardless of your feelings for weak-link employees, they are a liability to the team, especially when things get busy. To be successful when it is busy, you rely on all team members to be able to carry their weight. When they don't, others must pick up the slack, which is more responsibility for them than is fair. This causes tension. Yes, people develop and learn at different rates, but mistakes must not recur.

As a manager, you probably went by gut feeling when you promoted or hired this employee and knew that he or she might need extra training. But a manager needs to see progress and to never tolerate regression. When that happens, the decision must be swift. Managers cannot jeopardize their primary function of building a team for success in the business. A weak link must be either demoted or let go. Sometimes a manager's gut feeling is wrong. Admit the mistake, cut the losses, and move on.

These two employee types contribute to the fragileness of the restaurant environment. You cannot tolerate B and C players, which is what the "won'ts" and "can'ts" are. These are not necessarily toxic employees, but they will not enable a business to thrive. The weak-link employee can't contribute, and the slacker won't contribute. These each bring down morale in their own way. The slacker purposefully neglects duties, and the overwhelmed employee can't even accomplish her or his own duties, let alone pitch in and help. Both scenarios will frustrate your A players, who want all their peers to be at the same level of work ethic and ability.

Now here's an employee type that is toxic, directly influencing the culture in a negative way: the bully. Every business in every industry has witnessed these. According to a 2014 survey by the Workplace Bullying Institute, 38 percent of coworkers who witnessed bullying at the workplace did nothing. Nothing! Of the 29 percent who did come forth and help, there was another obstacle. Gary Namie and his team found in their study that when managers were approached about in-house bullying, their response was negative 72 percent of the time (Namie 2014). Managers either denied that it had occurred or discounted incidents as no big deal, especially if the offender was another manager. Unfortunately, in more than half of cases, the bully is a manager.

I've observed bullies who were supervisors and non-supervisors. A bullying supervisor relishes control. His or her authority and hunger for control is fed by belittling and humiliating the staff. The bully enjoys publicly humiliating others for all to witness. The bullying supervisor manages with fear. A nonsupervisory bully is a manipulator who just needs a few other employees to create a little pocket of negativity. Bullies prey on timid employees with verbal assaults that assert the superiority of the bully and try to trip up and upset the victim, usually when the stress of the business is running high.

These are just a few examples of how bullying can rear its ugly head. One thing is for certain—if there is bullying in any capacity, in any position, there is no chance of establishing a positive culture. The bully must go. Where a leader jumps in and helps a team member, the bully will do or say anything to see the victim fail. A bully is a leader's polar opposite! Once bullying behavior has been identified, swift action needs to be taken.

## The Baby-Blanket Syndrome

Decisions about employees become difficult when emotions are involved. This is especially true for a manager who must make decisions concerning a long-standing employee. Over time, conversations at work become more personal, and managers develop emotional connections with staff members. Both managers and long-standing employees see many coworkers come through, with the high turnover rate in the restaurant industry. A manager and a long-standing employee have many experiences together over the years. The relationship can become so strong that any disciplining of such an employee becomes difficult. I refer to this scenario as the "baby-blanket syndrome."

This dilemma is similar to what parents encounter when they want to remove a baby blanket or other emotional crutch from a child. It can be any object of familiarity that a child reaches for when he or she feels stressed because of fear, change, or just being alone. For a manager, the baby blanket is not a familiar object but a familiar person who, over the years, has turned negative and must be removed. Attempts are made to change this individual, but they are unsuccessful. Just as parents might look at the blanket and remember its history—a stain from a year earlier, for example, or a rip that they tried to repair, or frayed edges—the blanket has reached the end of its life and must be removed. Yet it has now become a crutch for the child.

A manager may have a similar experience when confronting a longtime employee to discipline or even reprimand him or her for their attitude or actions; the employee has become bitter and resistant to change. Through the years, the manager has probably shared many experiences with this employee, both in the workplace and maybe even on a personal level. Well, people change over the years, and who once was dedicated, proactive, and an integral part of the business has, like the blanket, become rough around the edges. This employee might have lost patience when developing newer employees, but patience is crucial when teaching and developing people. The manager has probably noticed that this employee's attitude has soured over the years. This rip in the person's behavior does not usually happen overnight.

This is where managers must not allow any emotional connection to the employee to cloud their judgement. Managers must not allow any emotions to overshadow their ability or responsibility to make the decision that is in the best interest of the business. If managers are unable to accomplish this and keep putting the issue on the back burner, they are now also part of the problem! It is easier said than done to keep your decision objective, because there are personal feelings involved.

You might try to get through to the employee who has turned bitter and negative and get him or her to reengage. True management is not an easy job. Regardless of how difficult the decision is, your job as manager is to make sure that you do what is best for the business. This also underlines to the rest of the staff what you expect from it.

For a manager, patience is a necessary attribute when developing the staff. There will be errors along the way. You are teaching people, and they all develop at different rates. If you don't give each one a chance to blossom, you could potentially lose an amazing future employee. A manager should look for an employee's continued improvement, which shows that she or he is trying and taking the job seriously. Learning and development is an ongoing process. Repeated mistakes indicate a lack of focus or understanding. Chemistry between employees is very important for a team so that they work well together under pressure.

## THE FARM SYSTEM

Restaurants and the hospitality business are not for everyone. This is why there's an industry-wide problem of finding and keeping qualified employees. Even when you find people you think are qualified, some find that they don't like the business, or their performance is underwhelming. Again, don't overlook a current employee who might be a great candidate for promotion from within—that's a "farm system." You've heard the term used in pro sports, like baseball and hockey. A farm league is like a minor league that feeds players up to the major or professional league. Minor leagues are where newer players get training and experience until they are good enough to play in the major leagues. Restaurants and bars don't have minor leagues, but they can implement a farm system that recognizes performing employees and allows them to climb the ladder.

When you promote your entry-level positions, like host, busser, or server, the staff and management will need to be patient realizing whoever is in this new position, has no experience at it yet. But you know this employee's work ethic and attitude and that he or she has worked within the established culture. Within a supportive system, the newly promoted person can succeed. Managers can teach an employee everything about the job, like the POS system, steps of service, and the menu, but as I've mentioned, it's difficult to teach someone how to be nice and work within the system.

You can always hire an experienced applicant, hoping that he or she can contribute right away, with minimal training. Over the years, though, I have seen experienced employees bring their bad habits with them, and this can affect the rest of the staff.

Note that the farm system does not apply to all your employees but only to those who have proven themselves at their previous positions. The existing staff knows who has a good work ethic and a positive attitude just from day-to-day interaction. Those with good work ethics earn respect from other staff members. For the farm system to be successful, that respect must already exist. Without it, there is little chance that the existing staff will aid in the development of a former-host-turned-server, for example. The way to evaluate an employee is to ask whether you are better place with him or her or better off with a replacement. This approach takes your subjective feelings out of the decision-making process. This is business. Having a weak link or B or C player anywhere is not conducive to the growth and success of the business.

For the farm system to work, it takes discipline and cooperation from the team. It involves a longer development process, and that requires an entire team's effort—and therefore the proper culture. Your team, particularly the trainers, must be empowered to keep trainees in training if they're not ready to go it alone. If your trainer feels the trainee needs a few more training shifts, the managers should trust their judgment. The level of customer service depends on it. One of the greatest feelings for me is the joy of watching someone grow through the farm system and excel in a new position.

For managers to have any chance of inspiring the staff, first and foremost, they must be inspired themselves. They can't inspire, though, if they don't know how to communicate. They must put passion into their words and, even more important, their actions. How in the world can you inspire the team if you are not passionate yourself? Putting on a fake front and preaching respect and teamwork to the group and then being overheard talking trash about your team or policies creates a negative effect. Someone is always watching or listening, and you, as a manager, must always be a role model.

Here is the difference between driving and inspiring—pumping up your team for the game or the moment and getting them to stay focused. It's always down to respect and communication. When you are talking to your staff, try something different. Rather than trying to light a fire under someone's feet to get results, try lighting a candle inside someone's head. A leader can encourage the team to understand an order as well as the reason that it's necessary. A leader can influence staff to believe in his or her words and execute them automatically.

A boss drives the team to get things accomplished. Leaders don't have to do that. They set the example by practicing what they preach. The leader has just as much goodwill for the team's success as she or he does for the customer's satisfaction. Managers who have the "do as I say, not as I do" mentality have no chance of gaining respect from their team and becoming leaders.

> *Success is nothing more than a few simple disciplines, practiced*
> *every day; while failure is simply a few errors in judgement,*
> *repeated every day. It is the accumulative weight of our disciplines*
> *and our judgements that leads us to either success or failure.*

—JIM ROHN

Jim Rohn was an inspirational speaker whose description of the evolution of a leader sums it up perfectly. Learn the skills and knowledge to perform the task well, and then stay disciplined and perform it until it becomes a habit. In other words, know the job inside and out. And finally, once you master the job, you have to be able to teach it to someone new. Transfer your knowledge to develop others. A true leader is a teacher.

# ABOUT THE AUTHOR

● ● ●

NICK VLAHOS HAS OVER THIRTY years experience in the restaurant industry. His experience includes owning a small diner to managing multimillion-dollar businesses with over 150 employees.

Throughout his many years in the restaurant industry, the thing that has remained constant is his belief that a strong staff led by strong leadership is essential to the success of a restaurant no matter how large or how small.

Vlahos holds a bachelors degree in electrical engineering. He is married with three children. He also maintains a web presence at therestaurantmachineblog.com.

# REFERENCES

French's Mustard. 2014. "French's History." http://www.frenchs.com/our-story/.

Hayghe, Howard V. 1990. "Family Members in the Work Force." *Monthly Labor Review* (March). https://www.bls.gov/mlr/1990/03/art2full.pdf.

Olver, Lynne. 2000. "Food Timeline; Restaurants and Catering." http://www.foodtimeline.org/restaurants.html#foodservice.

Parsa H. G., J. Self, D. Njite, and T. King. 2005. "Why Restaurants Fail." Cornell Hotel and Restaurant Administration Quarterly 46 (3). doi:10.1177/0010880405275598.

Namie Gary. 2014. "2014 WBI Workplace Bullying Survey, February 2014." http://www.workplacebullying.org/wbiresearch/wbi-2014-us-survey/.

National Hot Dog and Sausage Council. 2016. "Hot Dog History." http://www.hot-dog.org/culture/hot-dog-history

US Department of Labor, Bureau of Labor Statistics. 2017. "Employment Characteristics of Families—2016." https://www.bls.gov/news.release/pdf/famee.pdf.

Restaurant Opportunities Centers United, Forward Together, et al. October 7th, 2014. The Glass Floor: Sexual Harassment in the Restaurant Industry. New York, NY: Restaurant Opportunities Centers United. http://rocunited.org/wp-content/uploads/2014/10/REPORT_TheGlassFloor_Sexual-Harassment-in-the-Restaurant-Industry.pdf

————. 2017. "Industries at a Glance: Food Services and Drinking Places." https://www.bls.gov/iag/tgs/iag722.htm.

————. 2017. "Occupational Employment Statistics." https://www.bls.gov/oes/current/oes350000.htm.

Made in the USA
Middletown, DE
13 May 2019